Catherine's
FAMILY KITCHEN

CATHERINE FULVIO

Gill & Macmillan

Gill and Macmillan
Hume Avenue, Park West, Dublin 12
with associated companies throughout the world
www.gillmacmillan.ie

© Catherine Fulvio, 2011
978 07171 5057 1

Photography by Joanne Murphy
Styled by Orla Neligan
Assistant to photographer and stylist: Carly Horan

Props supplied by Ballyknocken Cookery School; Avoca: HQ Kilmacanogue, Bray, Co. Wicklow,
T: (01) 2746939, E: info@avoca.ie, www.avoca.ie; Meadows & Byrne: Dublin, Cork, Galway, Clare,
Tipperary, T: (01) 2804554/(021) 4344100, E: info@meadowsandbyrne.ie,
www.meadowsandbyrne.com; Marks & Spencer: Dundrum Town Centre, Dundrum, Dublin 14,
T: (01) 2991300, www.marksandspencer.com; Cath Kidston: Unit CSD 1.3, Dundrum Shopping
Centre, Dundrum, Dublin 14, T: (01) 2964430, E: welovetolisten@cathkidston.com,
www.cathkidston.co.uk; Seagreen: 11a–12a The Crescent, Monkstown, Co. Dublin,
T: (01) 2020130, E: info@seagreen.ie, www.seagreen.ie;
Eden Home & Garden: 1–4 Temple Grove, Temple Road, Blackrock, Co. Dublin, T: (01) 7642004,
edenhomeandgarden@hotmail.com, www.edenhomeandgarden.ie;
A La Campagne: 31 Main Street, Gorey, Co. Wexford, T: (053) 9481450.
Index compiled by Cover to Cover
Book design and typesetting by Anú Design, Tara
Printed by Printer Trento SpA, Italy

This book is typeset in URWGrotesk Light, 10.5pt on 14.5pt.

The paper used in this book comes from the wood pulp of managed forests.
For every tree felled, at least one tree is planted, thereby renewing natural resources.

A CIP catalogue record for this book is available from the British Library.

5 4 3 2 1

To Charlotte and Rowan

My little angels ... most of the time!

With love,

Mum x

Acknowledgements

Thank you to my husband, Claudio, children, Charlotte and Rowan, my dad, Charlie, and all of my huge family for your continuous support. Without your love, books would not be written.

Thank you to my family at work, Sharon, Rowena, Aoife, Gema and Mary, for putting up with me when it gets hot in the kitchen!

Thank you Aoife and Aileen for flying the flag so well.

Thank you to Jo, Roisin and Sean – you are supermodels and great friends! Jo, you look great on the cover.

Thanks to Orla and Jo for your Trojan work in making the food look so good.

Thank you to all at Gill & Macmillan, especially Fergal, Ciara, Nicki, Catherine, Kristin, Teresa, Paul and Peter. Your dedication is inspirational.

Thank you to my extended family at RTÉ Cork and Dublin, especially Colm and Marie, and thank you to UKTV Food for your guidance.

And finally, thank you to all of our guests at Ballyknocken House and Cookery School. Your support is invaluable.

Catherine x

Contents

Soups and Starters

Breads and Baking

Speedy Suppers

Meat and Fish

Vegetable and Potato Sides

BBQ, Salads and Picnics

Desserts

Five Quick Sauces for Sweets

Drinks

Index

Introduction

It could be argued that the definition of family happiness depends on who has possession of the TV remote, and sometimes, in the Fulvio household, that truly is the case. But we are all in agreement when it comes to food. There is nothing quite like sitting around the dinner table, laughing, joking, catching up and, most importantly, enjoying good home-cooked food.

I believe that as a mother, one of my responsibilities is to create great memories for my children so that when they grow up, they can tell their children about the amazing, fun childhood they had. I really think that Charlotte and Rowan will remember the wonderful times and fabulous food we have had at BBQs, birthday parties and picnics with our extended family.

Between the Sicilian side of the family and the Wicklow crew, we have a very large family. All cousins are around the same age too, as are nieces and nephews, so in all it makes for fantastic social gatherings. Being surrounded by the people you grew up with feels like a warm security blanket and we always make time for each other. But before I am overcome with soppiness, let me tell you a little about the recipes in the book!

The recipes are specially developed as everyday dishes with a twist. Just like every other parent, I know what it feels like to dash into the kitchen, whip open the fridge door and search for inspiration as hungry children make their feelings known in the background. And I love entertaining, having friends and family around for little parties – or big ones, for that matter! – but I make sure that I enjoy the moment and am careful not to let myself get stressed in the kitchen. I believe that recipes should be doable, uncomplicated, interesting and, most importantly, very tasty! I hope you enjoy the recipes as much as I enjoyed writing and testing them.

Warmest wishes from a cosy kitchen,
Catherine x

Store Cupboard Essentials

Flour – plain, wholemeal and '00' or strong white flour

Porridge oats

Sugar – caster sugar and brown sugar

Bread soda (bicarbonate of soda)

Baking powder

Ground cinnamon

Nutmeg

Vanilla beans

Honey

Almonds – whole and flaked

72% bittersweet chocolate

Tinned cherries

Oil – extra virgin olive oil, a light olive oil, sunflower or vegetable oil

Mustard – Dijon, wholegrain and mustard powder

Vinegar – red wine, balsamic

Soy sauce

Thai fish sauce (*nam pla*)

Thai red curry paste

Dried chillies

Chilli powder or flakes

Ground cumin

Ground coriander

Curry powder

Paprika

Dried oregano

Garlic salt

Sea salt

Black pepper

Rice – basmati, long grain and Arborio

Pasta – fettuccine, penne, fusilli, farfalle

Lentils

Kidney beans

Pine nuts

Canned tomatoes – plum, cherry and passata

Tomato purée

Sundried tomatoes

Jars of olives

Pesto

Five Useful Gadgets

1 **Microplane:** The school and my home couldn't be without one. It's an essential in every kitchen. Zesting limes and lemons is a dream – no beating the grater or trying to get little bits out with the knife!

2 **Meat thermometer:** Always a must for safely cooking meat, especially for barbecuing.

3 **Pestle and mortar:** Pesto made in a pestle and mortar is the best, as are marinades and rubs. It allows you to combine wonderful flavours with great texture.

4 **Ricer:** My reliable and favourite item, it produces the most fabulous fluffy mashed potatoes.

5 **Mandolin:** The easy way out to dice and slice sweet potatoes or cut carrots paper thin. Just remember to use the safety guard!

Five Ways with Chopping

1 **Finely chopped:** Small, even-sized pieces between 4mm and 5mm. Many herbs and chillies are chopped finely for pasta or in sauces.

2 **Medium dice:** To cut into small cubes about 7mm in size, e.g. red peppers for a salsa.

3 **Slice:** Evenly cut about 2mm to 3mm thick, e.g. onion rings.

4 **Julienne (often called matchsticks):** Using your cook's knife, slice 4mm wide and about 4cm in length.

5 **Roughly diced:** Evenly cubed into 2cm to 3cm pieces. Use this for soups or recipes that use a food processor.

Soups and Starters

Five Quick Soups

Here are my five quick and tasty soups. As with all soups, first heat the saucepan over a high heat, add the oil and onions, shallots and/or leeks, reduce the heat to low and sauté for 7-8 minutes, until soft. Then add the harder vegetables, which are generally the root vegetables, e.g. potato or butternut squash, with the liquid, which is usually chicken or vegetable stock. When softened, add the leaf vegetables, e.g. sorrel or watercress. Then purée, season, garnish and serve.

1 Butternut Squash, Sage and Apple Soup

Serves 4

sunflower oil

2 medium onions, chopped

1 medium butternut squash, peeled, deseeded and diced

1 large cooking apple, peeled, cored and diced

1.5 litres chicken or vegetable stock, plus extra to thin the soup if required

1 tbsp fresh chopped sage

salt and freshly ground black pepper

sage leaves, to garnish

cream, to garnish

2 Spicy Sweet Potato and Coriander Soup

Serves 4

sunflower oil

1 large onion, sliced

2 garlic cloves, chopped

2 ripe tomatoes, chopped

2 tbsp Thai red curry paste (or to taste)

1 tsp cumin seeds

3 sweet potatoes, peeled and diced

1.2 litres chicken or vegetable stock

½ lemon, juice only

small handful of coriander leaves

salt and freshly ground black pepper

crème fraîche, to garnish

paprika, to garnish

naan bread, to serve

3 Watercress Soup with Parmesan Toast

Serves 4

extra virgin olive oil

1 leek, white part only, finely sliced

1 medium onion, finely chopped

2 large potatoes, peeled and diced small

1.5 litres chicken or vegetable stock

200g watercress

salt and freshly ground black pepper

4 small watercress sprigs, to garnish

To serve, brush 4 slices of ciabatta with extra virgin olive oil. Grill on both sides. Sprinkle with 2 tbsp Parmesan and place under the grill until golden.

4 Potato, Spinach and Sorrel Soup

Serves 4

extra virgin olive oil

4 shallots, peeled and sliced

2 leeks, white part only, finely sliced

2 garlic cloves, sliced

1 bay leaf

1 tsp chopped fresh thyme

4 large potatoes, peeled and sliced

1.5 litres chicken stock

200g baby spinach

10 large sorrel leaves

salt and freshly ground black pepper

2 tbsp cream, to garnish

5 Carrot and Beetroot Soup

Serves 4

extra virgin olive oil

3 carrots, peeled and chopped

2 celery stalks, chopped

2 beetroot, cooked, peeled and diced

1 onion, finely chopped

1 potato, peeled and diced

1.2 litres vegetable stock

½ orange, zest only

salt and freshly ground black pepper

2 tbsp sour cream, to garnish

chopped chives, to garnish

Red Lentil, Red Pepper and Coconut Soup

This soup is one of our most popular soups that we serve to our guests at Ballyknocken House. It's hearty and the flavours are well balanced. Red lentils are also inexpensive and easy to use, so we should make more use of them.

Serves 4

sunflower oil

1 onion, finely chopped

2 celery stalks, finely sliced

1 ½ red chillies, deseeded and finely chopped

2cm fresh ginger, grated

½ tsp ground cumin

2 red peppers, deseeded and diced

100g red lentils

1 x 400ml tin of coconut milk

400ml vegetable stock, plus extra to thin the soup if required

salt and freshly ground black pepper

toasted desiccated coconut, to serve

1. Heat a large saucepan over a high heat. Add the oil, onion and celery, reduce the heat to low and sauté for 7–8 minutes, until soft.
2. Add the chillies, ginger and cumin and cook for 1 minute more.
3. Add the peppers, lentils, coconut milk and stock and stir to mix. Continue to cook for about 10 minutes, until the peppers are soft.
4. Remove from the heat and allow to cool slightly. Using a hand blender, purée the soup until smooth.
5. Season to taste and reheat.
6. Sprinkle the toasted coconut over the soup to serve.

If you aren't a big fan of coconut milk, use half milk, half cream instead.

Roasted Yellow Pepper Soup and Tomato Soup

This soup has two parts and the two colours look great together. Just be careful when you serve them both in the same bowl that they don't merge together. If they do, just give them a swirl with a spoon and it will still look pretty.

Serves 4–6

For the yellow pepper soup:

4 yellow peppers

extra virgin olive oil

1 onion, finely diced

1 tsp chopped fresh thyme

250ml vegetable stock, plus extra to thin the soup if required

3 tbsp cream

salt and freshly ground black pepper

For the tomato soup:

extra virgin olive oil

2 garlic cloves, sliced

2 sundried tomatoes, chopped

1 potato, peeled and diced

1 x 400g tin of chopped tomatoes

300ml vegetable stock, plus extra to thin the soup if required

2 tsp chopped fresh basil

salt and freshly ground black pepper

1. Preheat the oven to 180°C/fan 160°C/gas 4.
2. To make the yellow pepper soup, place the peppers on a roasting tray, rub with olive oil and roast for about 20 minutes, turning them over halfway through the cooking time, until the skin has blistered. Remove immediately from the oven, place in a plastic bag and seal.
3. After 30 minutes, remove the peppers from the bag and peel away the skin. Set aside.
4. Heat a large saucepan over a high heat. Add some oil and the onion, reduce the heat to low and sauté for 7–8 minutes, until soft.
5. Deseed and roughly chop the peppers. Add the peppers, thyme and stock to the onion and heat through.
6. Using a hand blender, purée the soup.
7. Add the cream and taste for seasoning, adding salt and pepper as required.
8. To make the tomato soup, heat a large saucepan over a medium heat. Add some oil, the garlic and sundried tomatoes and sauté for 1 minute.
9. Stir in the potato, tomatoes and stock and bring to a boil. Reduce the heat and simmer for 10–15 minutes, until the potato is cooked through. Add in the basil and remove from the heat.
10. Purée the soup and taste for seasoning.
11. To serve, using two ladles, pour one ladle each of yellow pepper and tomato soup into a bowl at the same time. They will stay separate for an amazing-looking and even better-tasting yellow pepper and tomato soup.

 Serve this soup with Parma Spiral Sticks (see p. 39).

Curried Chicken Coconut Noodle Soup

This recipe is from our Vietnamese class in our cookery school and has become a firm favourite in the Fulvio household. It is so hearty that it is wonderful as a main supper in the evening.

Serves 4–6

vegetable oil

1 large garlic clove, minced

2 tbsp curry powder

800ml–1 litre chicken stock

1 x 400ml tin of unsweetened coconut milk

100ml water

6 thin slices of fresh ginger

1 stalk of lemongrass, the woody top section discarded and the remainder minced

½ tsp whole black peppercorns

2 chicken breasts

130g medium Asian egg noodles

3 tbsp lime juice (about 1 ½ limes)

3 tbsp Thai fish sauce (*nam pla*)

1 sprig of fresh coriander, chopped

1. Heat a saucepan over a moderately low heat. Add some oil and the garlic and stir for 1 minute, until it's fragrant. Add the curry powder and cook for 30 seconds.
2. Stir in the stock, coconut milk, water, ginger root, lemongrass and peppercorns. Bring the mixture to a simmer. Add the chicken and poach it for about 20 minutes, or until it's cooked through.
3. Transfer the chicken to a plate. Using two forks, shred the chicken and stir it back into the broth.
4. Add the noodles to the soup, stir to soften and simmer for about 3 minutes, taking care not to overcook.
5. Add the lime juice and the Thai fish sauce. Taste for seasoning, adding more Thai fish sauce or lime juice as required.
6. Using a tongs, divide the noodles among the bowls and ladle the soup over them. Sprinkle with coriander and serve.

❋ If freezing this soup, omit the noodles, as these can be added in when reheating. They only take a few minutes to cook in the broth.

Chicken, Sweetcorn and Green Chilli Chowder

First, this is my take on fast food. Second, it has all the food groups – it's my one-pot wonder guaranteed to please all the family.

Serves 4

30g butter

2 leeks, thinly sliced

1 large green chilli, deseeded and diced

2 chicken breasts, diced small

2 large sweet potatoes, peeled and diced

500ml chicken stock

400ml milk

200ml cream

1 tbsp chopped fresh coriander, plus extra to garnish

175g frozen sweetcorn

salt and freshly ground black pepper

crusty bread, to serve

1. Heat a large saucepan over a high heat. Add the butter, leeks and chilli, reduce the heat to very low and sauté for 5–7 minutes, until softened but not brown.
2. Add the chicken, sweet potatoes, stock, milk, cream and coriander and simmer for 8–10 minutes. Stir in the sweetcorn and simmer for a further 3 minutes. Season with salt and pepper to taste.
3. Serve with a sprinkle of chopped coriander and crusty bread.

Try replacing the chicken with smoked haddock and adding 3 tbsp peas.

Thai-style Crab Cakes with a Spicy Sesame Dipping Sauce

I love themed parties, especially a Thai-style evening, and this is my favourite starter. It's easy, tasty and can be prepared ahead to the point of sautéing the cakes, which leaves more time for mixing the cocktails!

Serves 4 (makes 12 x 5cm round cakes)

For the crab cakes:

2 spring onions, roughly chopped

1 tbsp Thai red curry paste

½ lime, zest and juice

1cm piece of fresh ginger, peeled and roughly chopped

1 tbsp fresh coriander leaves, plus a few sprigs to garnish

2 tsp Thai fish sauce (*nam pla*)

150g crabmeat

150g mashed potatoes

3 tbsp lightly seasoned plain flour

1 egg beaten with a little milk

100g breadcrumbs, seasoned with salt and pepper

sunflower oil

For the dipping sauce:

2 tbsp lime juice

1 tbsp sesame oil

1 tbsp soy sauce

1 ½ tsp Thai fish sauce (*nam pla*)

1 tsp caster sugar

1 tsp sesame seeds, toasted

1 medium red chilli, deseeded and finely chopped

50ml water

fresh coriander leaves, to garnish

lime slices, to garnish

Oriental Salad, to serve (see p. 135)

1. To make the crab cakes, place the spring onions, Thai red curry paste, lime zest and juice, ginger, coriander leaves and Thai fish sauce in a small food processor and blend to a paste.

2. Transfer the mixture to a mixing bowl. Add the crabmeat and mashed potatoes and mix well. To check for seasoning, fry a mini cake and adjust seasoning to taste.

3. Shape to form 12 cakes. Keep them in the refrigerator until needed.

4. Meanwhile, make the dipping sauce by combining all of the ingredients in a bowl.

5. To cook the cakes, first coat them in the seasoned flour, shaking off any excess flour. Dip them in the beaten egg, then coat in the breadcrumbs. Heat a frying pan over a high heat, then add the oil and reduce the heat to medium. Fry the cakes gently on each side until they're a pale golden colour and fully cooked through. You will need to cook them in batches, adding a little more oil if necessary.

6. Serve with the dipping sauce and Oriental Salad (see p. 135). Garnish with some coriander and a slice of lime.

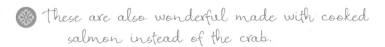 *These are also wonderful made with cooked salmon instead of the crab.*

Marinated Aubergine and Courgette with Soft Goat's Cheese and Hazelnut Dressing

For colour and flavour, I would give this recipe a 10 out of 10! I often prepare this for lunch for my girlfriends and I sometimes add roasted peppers, olives and artichoke hearts for a very substantial salad.

Serves 4

2 large courgettes, sliced lengthways into 1cm-thick slices

1 large aubergine, sliced lengthways into 1cm-thick slices

extra virgin olive oil

salt and freshly ground black pepper

200g soft goat's cheese

2 tbsp hazelnuts, roasted and roughly chopped

2 tbsp finely chopped fresh flat-leaf parsley

For the dressing:

3 tbsp extra virgin olive oil

1 tbsp hazelnut oil

½ lemon, zest and juice

1 tbsp finely chopped fresh flat-leaf parsley

1 tsp sugar

salt and freshly ground black pepper

1. Heat a griddle pan until very hot. Brush the courgettes and aubergine with a little oil, season with salt and pepper and fry in batches until soft and cooked through. Arrange on a platter.
2. To make the dressing, place all the ingredients in a sealed jar and shake to emulsify. Drizzle over the vegetables.
3. Let the flavours blend for 5 minutes, then scatter the goat's cheese, hazelnuts and parsley over the top and serve.

It's best to buy hazelnuts whole and still in their skins. To remove the skins, roast the nuts on a dry roasting pan in the oven at 200°C/fan 180°C/gas 6 until the skins are bloated and start to crack. Remove the nuts and place them in a clean tea towel. Gather the four corners of the towel and rub the hazelnuts. This will release the skins.

Cashel Blue, Walnut and Grape Bruschetta Salad

This salad is a wonderful combination of textures and flavours. The sweetness of the grapes works so well with the saltiness of the cheese.

Serves 4

For the dressing:

1 large lemon, zest and juice

1 tbsp honey

salt and freshly ground black pepper

120ml extra virgin olive oil

For the bruschetta:

8 x 1 ½cm-thick slices of ciabatta, sliced diagonally

extra virgin olive oil, for brushing

1 large garlic clove, peeled and halved

For the salad:

250g mixed lettuce leaves

250g black grapes, halved lengthwise

200g Cashel Blue cheese, crumbled

6 cherry tomatoes

10 walnut halves, toasted and roughly chopped

1. Remove the zest from the lemon in large strips with a vegetable peeler and cut into thin strips. Blanch the zest in boiling water for 1 minute. Drain in a sieve, run under the cold tap and pat dry.
2. To make the dressing, whisk together the lemon juice, honey and salt and pepper in a jug. Slowly whisk in the oil until emulsified.
3. To prepare the ciabatta, brush both sides of the bread with some oil. Toast both sides under a grill until lightly golden in colour. Rub one side of the bread with the cut side of the garlic clove.
4. When ready to serve, toss the mixed lettuce leaves with the grapes, half of the lemon zest and enough salad dressing to coat. Put one slice of ciabatta on each salad plate and spoon 1 teaspoon of the remaining dressing over each. Layer the salad leaves on top.
5. Repeat with a second slice of ciabatta and place dressing and salad on top of that. Scatter the Cashel Blue on top. Place three tomato halves around the ciabatta. Sprinkle with the walnuts and the remaining lemon zest.

This salad dressing keeps for up to 2 weeks in the fridge, so make it in bulk!

Wild Mushroom, Lemon and Thyme Risotto

I adore wild mushrooms and we are lucky to live on a farm beside Carrick Forest here in Wicklow, which is mushroom heaven for foragers like me, but you need to know what you are looking for!

Serves 4

60g butter

200g wild mushrooms, brushed and chopped

1 lemon, zest only

2 tsp chopped fresh thyme

3 shallots, finely chopped

2 garlic cloves, chopped

300g Arborio rice

200ml white wine

1 litre vegetable or chicken stock

4 tbsp mascarpone

salt and freshly ground black pepper

1. Melt half the butter in a large saucepan. Add the mushrooms, lemon zest and thyme and sauté gently for about 5 minutes, until the mushrooms are fully cooked. Remove the mushroom mix and set aside.

2. Add the remaining butter to the saucepan and cook the shallots for 5 minutes. Add the garlic and cook for a further 2 minutes.

3. Add the rice and stir well until coated. Add the wine, stir and simmer for about 2 minutes.

4. Place the stock in a separate saucepan over a simmering heat. Add one ladle of the stock to the rice and stir gently until the stock is absorbed.

5. Continue to add the stock a ladle at a time, ensuring the rice has absorbed the stock before adding more, until all the stock is gone and the rice is cooked and 'al dente' – firm to the bite.

6. Return the mushrooms to the risotto and warm through. Stir in the mascarpone. Check for seasoning, adding salt and pepper to taste, and serve immediately.

For a lighter result, replace the mascarpone with cream.

Lemon Prawn Gratin

The ultimate quick and easy, yet impressive, recipe, this is a lovely starter when entertaining friends and family.

Serves 4

20 king prawns, peeled, tails on

60g butter, softened

2 garlic cloves, crushed

1 red chilli, deseeded and chopped

1 tbsp chopped fresh parsley

1 lemon, juiced

2 drops of Tabasco (or to taste)

salt

100g breadcrumbs

50g freshly grated Parmesan

1. Preheat the oven to 200°C/fan 180°C/gas 6.
2. Remove the tract from the prawns, then butterfly them by making an incision down the back of the prawn without cutting through. This will enable you to open it out.
3. Combine the butter, garlic, chilli, parsley, lemon juice and Tabasco and season with salt.
4. Divide the prawns between 4 individual gratin dishes and spread the flavoured butter over them. Mix the breadcrumbs and Parmesan together and sprinkle over the prawns.
5. Bake in the oven for 6–8 minutes, until the prawns are pink and the breadcrumbs are golden. Serve immediately.

Add some sautéed Irish bacon lardons to the prawns, yum!

Beetroot-cured Side of Salmon with Dill Potatoes

This salmon has a magical purple hue from the beetroot. We are blessed in Ireland to have wonderful fish available to us and salmon is one of our favourites.

Serves 4

For the salmon:

2 tbsp fennel seeds

1 tbsp black peppercorns

175g light soft brown sugar

120g rock salt

small bunch of dill, chopped

2 medium beetroot

1.2kg side of fresh Irish salmon, skinned and boned

For the dill potatoes:

extra virgin olive oil

1 small onion, finely chopped

1 garlic clove, finely chopped

3 large potatoes, diced

100ml cream

salt and freshly ground black pepper

2 tsp chopped fresh dill

1. Crush the fennel seeds and peppercorns in a pestle and mortar, then mix with the sugar and salt. Add half the dill to make a paste.
2. Grate the beetroot and add to the sugar and salt mixture.
3. Place the salmon in a non-metallic dish and rub the paste on both sides of the salmon. Cover with cling film. Put a baking tin on top and weigh down with some heavy weights (e.g. tins of beans). Leave in the fridge for at least 3 days, allowing time for curing and for the beetroot to colour the salmon.
4. Brush off the marinade, rinse the fish briefly under cold water and pat dry. Sprinkle with the remaining dill and chill until ready to serve.
5. To prepare the dill potatoes, heat a small saucepan over a high heat. Add some oil and the onion, reduce the heat to low and sauté for 5–7 minutes. Add the garlic and cook for a further 1 minute. Add in the potatoes and cover with the cream. Season with salt and pepper. Add the dill and simmer gently for 10–12 minutes, until the potatoes are cooked.
6. Check the seasoning, adding more salt and pepper as required. Serve hot with the beetroot-cured salmon.

 The potatoes make a lovely side dish with any fish for a main course.

Chicory, Radicchio, Chorizo and Wicklow Blue Cheese Salad

This is where I go local with cheese! John Hempenstall makes the most amazing artisan farmhouse cheeses at his nearby farm in Curranstown. I've used his Wicklow Blue here, but the recipe works with any local blue cheese.

Serves 6

200g chorizo, sliced and halved

150g crème fraîche

6 tbsp extra virgin olive oil

2 tbsp white wine vinegar

2 tbsp milk

2 heads chicory (Belgian endive), leaves separated and washed

1 head radicchio, leaves washed and torn

200g Wicklow Blue cheese, diced

1. Sauté the chorizo on a medium heat in a frying pan until golden and crispy. Remove with a slotted spoon and set aside.
2. In a bowl, whisk the crème fraîche, oil and vinegar until combined. Loosen with the milk.
3. Divide the chicory and radicchio between 6 plates. Drizzle the dressing over the leaves and scatter the cheese and chorizo over the top.

To impress your friends, serve this salad on a large platter and present it at the table so everyone can serve themselves.

Sundried Tomato and Pancetta Quiche with Parmesan Pastry

The Parmesan in the pastry gives this quiche a little twist. When entertaining, I love to make individual tartlets, as they are more impressive. If you don't like goat's cheese, you could use a soft Brie cheese instead.

Serves 6–8

200g plain flour, plus extra for dusting

100g butter, chilled and diced

2 tbsp grated Parmesan

½ tsp finely chopped fresh thyme

1 egg yolk, beaten

2–3 tbsp chilled water (you may need less)

For the filling:

4 sundried tomatoes, chopped

2 large eggs + 2 egg yolks

100g pancetta, cubed

150ml cream

100g crème fraîche

salt and freshly ground black pepper

100g soft goat's cheese

green salad, to serve

1. Preheat the oven to 180°C/fan 160°C/gas 4. Grease a 23cm flan tin with a removable base or 6 x 9cm tartlet tins.

2. Sieve the flour into a mixing bowl. Add the butter, Parmesan and thyme and rub them into the flour with your fingertips until the mixture resembles breadcrumbs.

3. Add the egg yolk and just enough water to form a dough. Wrap the dough in cling film and allow to rest in the fridge for 30 minutes.

4. On a floured surface, roll out the pastry until it's slightly larger than the tin. Line the tin with the pastry and trim the edges. Place a circle of parchment paper over the pastry and fill with baking beans.

5. Transfer to the oven and bake for 10 minutes. Remove the beans and paper and return to the oven for 2 minutes to crisp the base. Set aside.

6. For the filling, place all the ingredients except for the goat's cheese into a large bowl and mix gently. Pour the filling into the pastry case and divide the goat's cheese over the top.

7. Bake the quiche for 20–25 minutes, or until the filling is set. Serve warm or cold with a green salad.

 Bake your pastry case in advance and have it ready for the filling. A microplane grater is ideal for grating the Parmesan.

Breads and Baking

Five Ways
with White Soda Bread

I love the versatility of the traditional white soda bread recipe. Here are five suggestions on how to experiment with and enjoy this simple bread. I've brought some Italian influence to this recipe in the form of pesto pinwheels, focaccia and pizza to keep the other half happy!

1 Fresh Herb and Leek White Soda Bread

Makes 1 loaf

450g plain white flour

1 tsp caster sugar

1 tsp bread soda (bicarbonate of soda)

pinch of salt

1 large leek, white part only, finely diced and cooked until lightly caramelised

3 tbsp thyme, parsley and/or chives, chopped

350–400ml buttermilk

1. Preheat the oven to 200°C/fan 180°C/gas 6.
2. Sieve all the dry ingredients into a bowl. Mix in the cooked leek and the fresh herbs of your choice.
3. Make a well in the centre, pour in most of the buttermilk and mix with one hand to form a soft dough. If more buttermilk is needed, add it in now.
4. When mixed, turn the dough out onto a floured surface and knead lightly. Place on a floured baking tray and flatten gently. Make a fairly deep cross on the top.
5. Bake in the preheated oven for 15 minutes. Reduce the temperature to 180°C/fan 160°C/gas 4 and continue to bake for a further 20–25 minutes, or until golden brown and an inserted skewer comes out clean.
6. To test, tap the bottom of the loaf. If it sounds hollow, the bread is ready.

❋ Always mix with a light hand, not a wooden spoon. The lighter the mixing, the lighter the bread.

2 Pesto Pinwheels

Makes approximately 17 pinwheels

3 tbsp chopped black olives

3 tbsp chopped sundried tomatoes

1 jar of pesto

1. Preheat the oven to 200°C/fan 180°C/gas 6.
2. Using the standard white soda bread recipe on p. 33, omit the leeks and add the black olives and sundried tomatoes to the dry ingredients before adding the buttermilk.
3. Mix with one hand to form a soft dough, turn out onto a floured surface and flatten slightly. Using your rolling pin, roll out in a rectangular shape to about 1cm in height.
4. Spread the pesto over the top and roll the dough up like a Swiss roll, starting at the long side and rolling across.
5. Cut into slices about 2–2.5cm wide. Lie the slices flat on a floured baking tray and flatten slightly with your hand. Bake for 10–15 minutes. The baking time depends on the size of the pinwheels – they should be firm to touch and golden brown in colour.

3 Quick Soda Pizza

Makes 2 pizzas

2 tbsp grated cheddar cheese

thick tomato sauce

extra virgin olive oil

Topping options:

sliced chorizo or salami
bacon lardons
smoked chicken
sliced red or yellow peppers
cherry tomato halves
crumbled goat's cheese
sliced mozzarella cheese
blue cheese
artichoke hearts
anchovies
olives

1. Preheat the oven to 220°C/fan 200°C/gas 7.
2. Using the original soda bread recipe on p. 33, omit the leeks and add the grated cheese before adding the buttermilk.
3. Mix with one hand to form a soft dough and divide into 2 pieces.
4. Roll out each piece on a floured surface into 2 evenly sized circles. Place the circles on floured baking sheets.
5. Spoon tomato sauce on each pizza base, leaving a 1cm border just inside the circle. Brush this border with oil. Add a selection of toppings and bake for 15–20 minutes, until the dough is cooked through.

4 Flowerpot Soda Bread

Makes 3

vegetable oil

sunflower seeds

1 egg, beaten

You will also need three 10cm x 10cm unglazed terracotta flowerpots

To temper the pots:

1. First you need to temper the pots. This might seem like a lengthy process, but it only needs to be done once. Wash the pots really well in hot soapy water and leave to dry overnight.
2. Brush the pots with vegetable oil all around the inside, especially the lip. Repeat this process several times, as the pots are very absorbent.
3. Place the pots on a flat foil-lined baking sheet. Put the pots into a cold oven, then turn the oven on to 200°C/fan 180°C/gas 6. This allows the pots to warm up slowly and prevents cracking.
4. When the oven has reached the required temperature, turn it off again.
5. When you're ready to bake with the pots, oil them again.

To make the bread:

1. Preheat the oven to 200°C/fan 180°C/gas 6.
2. Prepare the Fresh Herb and Leek White Soda Bread recipe from p. 33 and divide the dough between the 3 flowerpots so that it reaches just below the lip of each pot. Brush with beaten egg and sprinkle with sunflower seeds or other seeds of your choice.
3. Bake for about 20 minutes, or until golden brown and an inserted skewer comes out clean. Leave them to rest in their pots for about 5 minutes before turning out on a cooking rack.

5 Soda Focaccia

Makes 1 loaf

2 tbsp sundried tomato purée

2 tbsp chopped sundried tomatoes

extra virgin olive oil

sea salt

Topping options:

grated Parmesan
sliced red onions
pitted olives
whole cherry tomatoes

1. Preheat the oven to 200°C/fan 180°C/gas 6.
2. Using the standard white soda bread recipe on p. 33, whisk the sundried tomato purée into the buttermilk. Omit the leeks from the original recipe and add the sundried tomatoes. Continue with the recipe until you form a soft dough.
3. Place into a well-oiled 21cm-square brownie tin. Dimple the top of the bread with your fingers, then add the toppings of your choice. Drizzle generously with extra virgin olive oil and sprinkle with sea salt.
4. Place in the preheated oven and bake for 15 minutes. Reduce the temperature to 180°C/fan 160°C/gas 4 and bake for a further 20–25 minutes, or until golden brown and an inserted skewer comes out clean. Cool on a wire rack before serving.

Ballyknocken Brown Bread

Every generation has their own version of brown soda bread. My grandmother, Kitty, made a traditional round loaf with a cross scored in it. My mother, Mary, broke family tradition by making hers in a loaf tin and this recipe is my version. It's quick and easy and very tasty.

Makes 1 loaf

225g self-raising white flour

225g stoneground coarse wholemeal flour

4 tbsp pinhead oatmeal, plus extra to decorate

4 tbsp sunflower or pumpkin seeds

2 tbsp bran

2 tbsp brown sugar

1 level tsp bread soda (bicarbonate of soda), sieved

pinch of salt

500ml natural yoghurt

150ml whole milk

1 tbsp sunflower oil

1. Preheat the oven to 200°C/fan 180°C/gas 6. Oil or line a 900g (2lb) loaf tin.
2. Mix the dry ingredients well in a bowl. Be sure to sieve the bread soda, as any lumps will result in green bread rather than brown bread!
3. Add the yoghurt, most of the milk and the oil and mix with one hand. Keep a little of the milk back, as the amount of milk depends on the thickness of the yoghurt – if the yoghurt is very thick, you will need the extra liquid to loosen the dough. The texture of the dough should be that of medium-thick porridge. When lifted up on a wooden spoon, it should plop off – if it doesn't fall off the spoon, add more milk. If it runs off the spoon, add more flour.
4. Spoon the mixture into the oiled loaf tin and sprinkle the extra oat flakes on top.
5. Place in the centre of the preheated oven and bake for 45–55 minutes. If the top of the bread is browning too quickly, turn down the oven slightly. The bread should be easy to remove from the loaf tin and should sound hollow when tapped underneath, which means it's cooked to perfection. Allow to cool and then serve.

Why not double up the recipe to make 2 loaves? The second loaf is always well received as a gift.

Parma Spiral Sticks

Little hands are useful for this recipe. My children love to shape these breadsticks. They are delicious for lunchboxes, but we adults love them with salads and soups.

Makes 16 sticks

1 ½ tsp sugar

1 rounded tsp dried yeast (or ½ x 7g sachet)

200ml lukewarm water (more if required)

350g '00' or strong white flour

1 tsp salt

1 ½ tbsp extra virgin olive oil, with extra for brushing

3 tbsp finely chopped sundried tomatoes

leaves from 2 rosemary sprigs, finely chopped

8 slices of Parma ham, sliced in half lengthways

1. Mix the sugar and yeast in the lukewarm water and allow the yeast to activate. When the yeast is frothy, it's ready to use.
2. Sieve the flour into a bowl and add the salt, olive oil and the yeast mixture. Mix to a soft dough with one hand, adding more flour or water as required. Knead on a floured surface until the dough is very pliable, which should take about 7–10 minutes by hand.
3. Leave the dough to rise in a well-oiled bowl covered with cling film until the dough has trebled in size and is springy to the touch, which will take about 2 hours. This will rise best in a warm, draught-free place, e.g. a hot press or near a cooker or oven.
4. When the dough is ready to shape, preheat the oven to 200°C/fan 180°C/gas 6. Line 2 baking trays with parchment paper.
5. Remove the dough from the bowl and lightly knead the sundried tomatoes and rosemary into the dough. Divide the dough into 16 small balls.
6. Roll each ball into a strip. Wind a slice of Parma ham along the length and twist them together. Transfer to a baking tray and repeat with the rest of the dough and Parma ham.
7. Brush each spiral stick with oil and bake in the oven for 12–15 minutes, or until golden.

For a vegetarian option, omit the Parma ham, brush with egg wash after twisting the dough and sprinkle with pine nuts.

39

Butternut Squash and Coriander Seed Bread

This is an unusual but unbelievably delicious and moist bread – the squash gives it a fabulous colour and the seeds add to the texture.

Makes 1 large loaf

1 small butternut squash (about 700g), cut into wedges

sunflower oil

salt and freshly ground black pepper

1 lemon, zest only

2 tbsp honey

1 tsp coriander seeds, lightly crushed, plus extra to decorate

2 ½ tsp dried yeast (or 1 x 7g sachet)

1 tsp sugar

280ml lukewarm water, more if required

650g '00' or strong white flour

½ tsp salt

1 egg, beaten

1. Preheat the oven to 180°C/fan 160°C/gas 4.
2. Place the butternut squash wedges in a lightly oiled roasting pan and drizzle with oil. Sprinkle with salt and pepper and roast for about 35 minutes, until golden and softened. Remove from the oven and set aside to cool. Once cooled, scoop the flesh from the skin and place in a bowl. Add the lemon zest, honey and coriander seeds and mash until smooth.
3. Mix the yeast and sugar in the lukewarm water and allow to activate. When the yeast is frothy, it's ready to use.
4. Meanwhile, sieve the flour and salt into a bowl. Add the yeast mixture as well as the butternut squash mixture, making sure you have enough liquid to form a soft dough. Knead on a floured surface for about 10 minutes, until smooth. Cover and leave in a warm place for about 2 hours, until it has doubled in size. The time will depend on the time of year and the temperature of the room.
5. Divide the dough into 2 pieces. Using the base of your hands, roll into two 30cm-long ropes.
6. Grease a baking tray with sunflower oil. Twist the ropes together, pinching them together at the ends. Cover and leave in a warm place until doubled in size, which should take about 1 hour.
7. Preheat the oven to 200°C/fan 180°C/gas 6.
8. Brush the loaf with the beaten egg and sprinkle with the coriander seeds. Bake for 25–30 minutes, until the bread sounds hollow when tapped on the bottom. Allow to cool on a cooling rack.

This moist bread has the most beautiful colour and should be enjoyed fresh on the day it's made. Otherwise, freeze it when it's fresh and it will keep for up to 3 months.

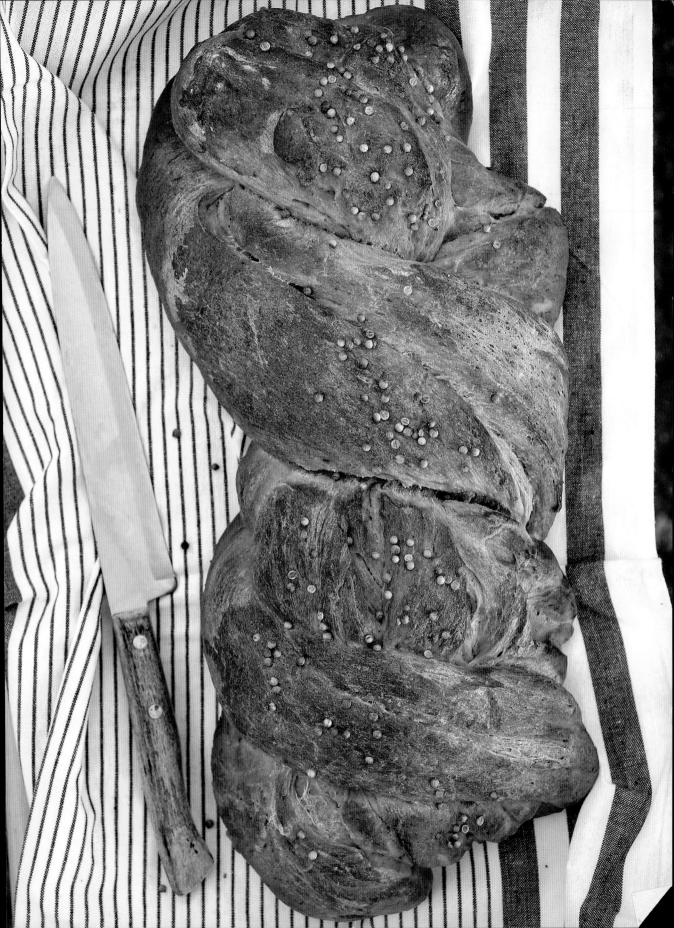

Guinness and Cranberry Bread

We couldn't come this far and not mention a recipe with Guinness in it! If I'm all out of cranberries, I simply use sultanas, which are equally as good in this recipe.

Makes 1 loaf

350g stoneground wholemeal flour

175g plain flour

100g dried cranberries

3 tbsp brown sugar

1 tsp bread soda (bicarbonate of soda), sieved

175ml Guinness

180ml buttermilk

pinch of salt

1. Preheat the oven to 200°C/fan 180°C/gas 6. Line a 900g (2lb) loaf tin with parchment paper.
2. Mix the dry ingredients well in a bowl, ensuring you get air into the flour by lifting it with your fingertips. Sieve the bread soda to ensure there are no lumps.
3. Add the Guinness and most of the buttermilk, adding more if required. Combine with a wooden spoon until the dough is a soft consistency.
4. Spoon the mixture into the prepared tin and flatten slightly. Bake in the preheated oven for 50 minutes, or until an inserted skewer comes out clean. If the bread is browning too quickly, reduce the oven temperature to 180°C/fan 160°C/gas 4 after 30 minutes.
5. When cooked, the bread should be well risen and should sound hollow when the base is tapped. Leave to cool on a wire rack.

Chilli Cornbread

Cornbread is so easy to make that you might be inclined to ask, 'What's the catch?' But there isn't any – it's easy, delicious and versatile. I slice the leftovers and use them as an alternative to ciabatta for bruschetta. Top with roasted red peppers and feta for a delicious result.

Makes 1 loaf

50g butter

150g self-raising flour

2 tsp baking powder

1 tsp salt

150g polenta (cornmeal)

1 tbsp caster sugar

½ tsp freshly ground black pepper

2 eggs, lightly beaten

300ml buttermilk

1 red chilli, deseeded and finely chopped

1. Preheat the oven to 180°C/fan 160°C/gas 4. Line a 900g (2lb) loaf tin with parchment paper.
2. Melt the butter in a saucepan and set aside.
3. Sieve the flour, baking powder and salt into a bowl. Add the polenta, sugar and pepper and mix well.
4. Make a well in the centre of the dry ingredients and quickly stir in the eggs, buttermilk and melted butter with a wooden spoon until you have a smooth, thick batter. Fold in the chilli until just combined.
5. Spoon the mixture into the prepared tin and bake for 45 minutes, or until golden brown and an inserted skewer comes out clean. Remove the loaf from the tin and place on a wire rack to cool. The loaf may be served warm or cold.

❀ Natural (unflavoured) yoghurt may be used as a substitute for buttermilk.

Five Ways
with Sweet Scones

To me, sweet scones always conjure up an image of dainty afternoon teas with roaring log fires and pretty teacups, but nowadays flavoured sweet scones are incredibly trendy, so move over cupcakes.

1 Sweet Scones

Makes approximately 17 scones

450g plain flour

2 tbsp caster sugar, plus extra to decorate

2 heaped tsp baking powder

pinch of salt

100g chilled butter, diced

280ml milk

1 egg, beaten

1. Preheat the oven to 220°C/fan 200°C/gas 7.
2. Sieve all the dry ingredients into a bowl. Using your fingertips, rub in the chilled butter until the mixture resembles fine breadcrumbs. Make a well in the centre and add most of the milk. Mix with one hand to form a soft dough, adding all of the milk if required.
3. Turn out onto a floured surface and knead lightly. Roll out the dough until it's approximately 2.5cm high.
4. Using a 5cm round scone cutter, cut the dough into circles as close together as possible. Gently reshape the leftover dough and cut out more scones.
5. Dip the top of the scones in the beaten egg and then in sugar. Place sugar side up on a floured baking tray.
6. Place in the oven immediately and bake for about 15 minutes, until the scones have risen and are golden on top.

2 Mango and Lime Scones

1 mango, peeled and diced

2 limes, zest only

1. Using the standard sweet scone recipe above, add the diced mango and lime zest to the mixture before adding the milk. Shape accordingly and bake.

47

3 Raspberry and Cinnamon Scones

80g fresh or frozen raspberries

½ tsp ground cinnamon

1. Using the standard sweet scone recipe on p. 47, add the raspberries and ground cinnamon before adding the milk. Shape accordingly and bake.

4 Pear, Ginger and Almond Scones

2 large ripe pears, peeled and diced

1 tbsp finely chopped crystallised ginger

½ tsp ground ginger

flaked almonds

1. Using the standard sweet scone recipe on p. 47, add the chopped pears, crystallised ginger and ground ginger before adding the milk. Shape accordingly. Glaze with the beaten egg, top with flaked almonds and bake.

5 Blueberry and White Chocolate Chip Scones

4 tbsp fresh or frozen blueberries

4 tbsp small white chocolate chips

1. Using the standard sweet scone recipe on p. 47, add the blueberries and white chocolate chips before adding the milk. Shape accordingly and bake.

Strawberry and Hazelnut Bread with Strawberry Butter

In the middle of the strawberry season here at Ballyknocken, when the berries are at their sweetest, I make this cake-style bread with my children. We also take it a step further by making strawberry butter, packing it all up and heading off to the nearby beach at Brittas Bay.

Makes 1 loaf

150g fresh strawberries, washed and hulled

350g self-raising flour

½ level tsp bread soda (bicarbonate of soda)

pinch of salt

175g golden caster sugar

100g butter, softened

2 eggs

75ml milk

75g hazelnuts, chopped

1. Preheat the oven to 180°C/fan 160°C/gas 4. Line a 900g (2lb) loaf tin with parchment paper.
2. Crush the strawberries and place in a small saucepan. Bring to a boil and simmer for 1 minute, stirring constantly. Remove from the heat and allow to cool.
3. In a medium bowl, combine the flour, bread soda and salt.
4. In a large bowl, using an electric whisk, cream the sugar and butter together. Gradually add the eggs and milk, mixing until light and fluffy.
5. Gently fold the flour mixture into the butter mixture until blended. Stir in the crushed strawberries and hazelnuts and spoon the mixture into the lined loaf tin.
6. Bake in the oven for 1 hour, or until a skewer inserted in the centre comes out clean. Leave the bread to cool in the tin for 10 minutes, then turn out onto a wire rack. Serve with the strawberry butter.

Strawberry Butter

200g butter, softened

120g fresh strawberries, washed and hulled

3 tbsp maple syrup

2 tbsp icing sugar

1. Place all the ingredients in a food processor and blend until smooth and creamy. Spoon into a ramekin and chill.

 Make strawberry muffins with this bread recipe by spooning the mixture into muffin cases instead. They should bake in 12-15 minutes.

Carrot Muffins with Lemon Frosting

I was going to call these Disappearing Muffins because as soon as I frost them, they just disappear. Apparently little and big hands are to blame.

Makes 12 muffins

For the muffins:

4 eggs

300g golden caster sugar

180ml sunflower oil

80ml milk

½ tsp vanilla extract

360g self-raising flour

1 tsp mixed spice

½ tsp salt

1 Granny Smith apple, peeled and diced small

200g grated carrots (3 medium carrots)

2 tbsp raisins, soaked in apple juice

For the lemon frosting (double the quantities if piping):

350g icing sugar, sieved

150g cream cheese

1 lemon, zest and a little juice

1. Preheat the oven to 180°C/fan 160°C/gas 4. Place muffin cases in the muffin tray.
2. Whisk the eggs, sugar, oil, milk and vanilla together in a bowl until thick and pale.
3. Fold in the flour, mixed spice and salt. Stir in the diced apple, grated carrots and raisins. Spoon the mixture into the muffin cases.
4. Bake for 20 minutes, or until golden. Place on a wire rack to cool fully before frosting.
5. To make the frosting, combine the icing sugar, cream cheese, lemon zest and just enough lemon juice to loosen the mixture, ensuring it's still thick enough to spread or pipe. Beat together well. Spread or pipe over the cooled cakes and enjoy.

 Use an ice cream scoop as a measure for the mixture.
If you don't have muffin cases, cut out 10cm squares of parchment paper and fold them into the muffin tray.

Speedy Suppers

Five Ways
with Speedy Pasta

My children would eat pasta for breakfast. That said, I try to limit it to lunch and dinner, so I find myself constantly experimenting to prepare pasta faster. What I love about pasta for a family meal is that it's quick and easy to prepare as well as filling and affordable. Here are five ideas that the adults will enjoy too!

In all of these recipes, cook the pasta according to the instructions on the packet and prepare the sauce in the meantime. Each recipe serves four.

1 Fettuccine with Smoked Salmon

300g fettuccine

extra virgin olive oil

6 spring onions, sliced

1 courgette, thinly sliced

150g smoked salmon, cut into strips

1 lemon, zest only

150ml cream

3 tbsp milk

1 tbsp chopped chives

salt and freshly ground black pepper

1. Heat a large pan over a high heat. Add some oil and the spring onions and courgette, reduce the heat to low and sauté for 7–8 minutes, until softened.
2. Add the smoked salmon, lemon zest, cream, milk and chives. Heat through, adding salt and pepper if required. Toss with the hot drained pasta and serve.

2 Spicy Cherry Tomato Penne with Prosciutto

300g penne

extra virgin olive oil

1 garlic clove, crushed

1 tbsp chopped fresh
flat-leaf parsley

1 tsp chopped fresh thyme

large pinch of chilli flakes
(to taste)

splash of white wine

250g cherry tomatoes

6 slices of prosciutto,
roughly chopped

1 tbsp pine nuts, toasted

salt and freshly ground
black pepper

2 tbsp grated Parmesan

1. Heat a large pan over a high heat. Add a generous
   amount of oil and the garlic, parsley, thyme and chilli
   flakes. Reduce the heat to low and sauté for 1–2 minutes.
2. Add the white wine and cherry tomatoes and sauté until
   the tomatoes burst. Add the prosciutto and pine nuts and
   cook for 1 minute more. Season with salt and pepper to
   taste.
3. Mix with the hot drained pasta, sprinkle with the
   Parmesan and serve immediately.

3 Lemon Pasta with Crème Fraîche and Rocket

300g tagliatelle

200g crème fraîche

2 lemons, zest (2 lemons)
and juice (½ lemon)

salt and freshly ground
black pepper

4 tbsp grated Parmesan

50g rocket

1. When straining the cooked pasta, retain 2 tbsp of the
   pasta cooking water. Return the pasta to the saucepan
   with the reserved water.
2. Add the crème fraîche, lemon zest and juice and season
   with salt and pepper to taste. Stir in the rocket, sprinkle
   over the Parmesan and serve.

4 Farfalle with Walnuts and Goat's Cheese

300g farfalle

100g soft goat's cheese

4 tbsp mascarpone cheese

2 tbsp chopped sundried tomatoes

¼ tsp grated nutmeg

salt and freshly ground black pepper

4 tbsp roughly chopped toasted walnuts

caramelised pear slices, to serve (optional)

1. When straining the cooked pasta, retain 2 tbsp of the pasta cooking water.
2. Place the reserved water, cheeses, sundried tomatoes, nutmeg, salt and pepper in a large saucepan and stir over a low heat.
3. Add the drained pasta and walnuts to the pan, stirring to coat the pasta well. Season with salt and pepper to taste and serve with caramelised pear slices.
4. To caramelise pears, halve, core and slice pears into wedges about 2cm in their thickest part. Heat a frying pan and add 50g butter and 2 tbsp brown sugar. Add the pears and sauté over a low heat, turning when browned on one side.

5 Mediterranean Roasted Vegetable Pasta

3 garlic cloves, finely sliced

2 courgettes, halved and cut into 3cm lengths

1 red pepper, roughly diced

1 yellow pepper, roughly diced

1 aubergine, diced

2 tbsp extra virgin olive oil

1 tbsp balsamic vinegar

1 tsp chopped fresh thyme

salt and freshly ground black pepper

300g pasta shells

180g crème fraîche

100g Gruyère, grated

1. Preheat the oven to 200°C/fan 180°C/gas 6.
2. Place the garlic, courgettes, peppers and aubergine into a roasting pan. Drizzle with the oil and balsamic vinegar and sprinkle over the thyme. Season with salt and pepper and roast for about 25 minutes, until the vegetables are tender and beginning to brown.
3. Meanwhile, cook and drain the pasta.
4. Stir the roasted vegetables into the pasta along with the crème fraîche. Check the seasoning, adding more salt and pepper if required. Sprinkle over the grated Gruyère and serve immediately.

Enchiladas with Tomato, Mild Chilli Sauce and Avocado Salad

What a great family favourite! I keep a batch of the tomato sauce in the freezer and one in the fridge to put a quick pasta meal on the table for my 'junior chefs'.

Serves 4

For the tomato sauce:

sunflower oil

1 onion, finely chopped

1 garlic clove, finely chopped

600g chopped tomatoes

1 carrot, grated

½ red chilli, finely chopped

2 tsp tomato purée

1 tsp sugar

salt and freshly ground black pepper

For the enchiladas:

175g cheddar cheese, grated, plus extra for the topping

8 tortillas

400g cooked chicken, cut into small strips or shredded

5 spring onions, finely sliced

150ml sour cream

For the salad:

4 radishes, sliced

1 avocado, peeled and diced

iceberg lettuce, thinly sliced

1 lemon, juice only

salt and freshly ground black pepper

1. First prepare the tomato sauce. Heat a saucepan on a high heat. Add some oil and the onion, reduce the heat to low and sauté the onion for 7–8 minutes, until softened. Add the garlic and cook for a further 2 minutes.
2. Stir in the tomatoes, grated carrot, chilli, tomato purée and sugar. Simmer gently, uncovered, for 12–14 minutes. Season with salt and pepper and set aside.
3. Preheat the oven to 180°C/fan 160°C/gas 4. Brush a wide, shallow ovenproof dish with a little oil.
4. Set aside 100ml of the tomato sauce and 4 tbsp of the grated cheese. Lay each tortilla out flat and spread some of the remaining tomato sauce over each one, followed by some chicken, spring onions, grated cheese and sour cream. Roll up and place seam side down in the dish. Pour over the retained sauce and sprinkle over the retained cheese. Bake for 20–25 minutes, until the top is golden.
5. Meanwhile, make the salad by combining the radishes, avocado and lettuce and drizzling over the lemon juice, tossing well. Season with salt and pepper to taste. Serve with the enchiladas.

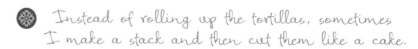 Instead of rolling up the tortillas, sometimes I make a stack and then cut them like a cake.

Roast Chicken, Avocado and Cheese Omelette

Sometimes, after a busy day, I just want to make a simple but tasty supper. An omelette ticks all the boxes for me and it can be dressed up to make an interesting meal. Here I have used chicken and avocado – delicious!

Serves 4 as a light supper

30g butter

5 eggs, free-range and organic if possible

1 tbsp milk

salt and freshly ground black pepper

150g roast chicken, shredded

4 slices of Emmental cheese

1 large avocado, peeled, stoned and thinly sliced

green salad, to serve

1. Heat a non-stick frying pan over a medium heat and add the butter.
2. Whisk the eggs and milk together in a bowl. Add a little salt and pepper and pour into the pan.
3. Using a rubber spatula, pull the egg to the centre and tilt the pan, allowing the unset egg to spread around the edge. When the mixture is almost set, add the shredded chicken, cheese and avocado. Add salt and pepper to taste.
4. Flip one half of the omelette over and slide onto a plate. Serve with a seasonal green salad.

If the omelette isn't setting on top, place it under the grill. The cheese melts and browns quickly this way too.

Honey-glazed Chicken Wings with a Blue Cheese Dipping Sauce

You will be making more than 16! Serve these with drinks before the main course. You'll need loads of napkins for the sticky fingers!

Serves 4

For the marinade:

2 garlic cloves, finely chopped

1 lemon, zest and juice

4 tbsp tomato ketchup

3 tbsp balsamic vinegar

2 tbsp honey

1 tbsp dark brown sugar

1 tbsp soy sauce

2 tsp paprika

¼ tsp Tabasco sauce

For the blue cheese dipping sauce:

150g cream cheese

100g blue cheese, such as Gorgonzola or Cashel Blue, rind removed and cheese diced

100ml sour cream

3 tbsp milk

1 tbsp chopped fresh chives

salt and freshly ground black pepper

For the wings:

16 chicken wings

extra virgin olive oil

salt and freshly ground black pepper

1. Combine all the marinade ingredients in a bowl and divide between 2 large Ziploc bags. Put 8 chicken wings in each bag and place in the fridge for 2–3 hours, turning occasionally. They can also be prepared the night before and left in the fridge overnight.
2. Preheat the oven to 180°C/fan 160°C/gas 4.
3. Place the wings on an oiled tray and roast for 10–12 minutes, turning once halfway through the cooking time. Check that the wings are fully cooked through before serving.
4. To make the dipping sauce, place the cream cheese, blue cheese and sour cream in a food processor and blend. Add the milk to adjust the consistency. Stir in the chives and add salt and pepper to taste.
5. Serve the wings with the blue cheese dipping sauce.

✽ Sprinkle 2 tbsp toasted sesame seeds over the wings before serving, omit the blue cheese and add 2 tbsp tahini to the dipping sauce.

Family-friendly Chicken Pasta Bake

'The dinner's in the oven' is a phrase I love. My mum used to say it when my brothers, sister and I would rush in from having spent a few hours helping Dad on the farm and we would be absolutely starving. Mum would lift a huge one-pot dish from the oven, place it on the table and we would ravenously dig in. In this case, the dinner's in the oven and it's a great way to use leftover chicken and vegetables!

Serves 4

200g fusilli

200g cooked chicken, diced

8 broccoli florets, blanched

5 tbsp frozen peas

For the white sauce:

4 tbsp butter

4 tbsp flour

600ml milk

100g white cheddar, grated

½ tsp Dijon mustard

salt and freshly ground black pepper

For the topping:

50g white cheddar, grated

4 tbsp breadcrumbs

1 tsp chopped fresh parsley

1. Preheat the oven to 180°C/fan 160°C/gas 4.
2. Cook the pasta in a large saucepan according to the instructions on the packet.
3. To make the sauce, melt the butter over a low heat in a saucepan large enough to accommodate the cooked pasta. Add the flour and cook for 2 minutes. Gradually whisk in the milk and allow it to thicken. Add the cheese and mustard and salt and pepper to taste.
4. Add the cooked, drained pasta to the sauce, followed by the chicken, broccoli and peas. Transfer to a greased ovenproof dish and sprinkle over the cheddar cheese, breadcrumbs and parsley. Bake for about 20 minutes, until golden brown.

 Try this with roasted courgettes and diced butternut squash. Omit the chicken for a vegetarian alternative.

Leek, Bacon and Broccoli Tortilla

Martha, Mabel and Marilyn, our hens, provide us with wonderful eggs. This is a great one-pan dish that is also delicious cold – I pack it for the children's school lunch.

Serves 4–6

extra virgin olive oil

2 leeks, finely sliced

4 pieces of rindless streaky bacon, sliced into lardons

6 eggs, free-range and organic if possible

2 large sundried tomatoes, chopped

4 tbsp grated mature Irish cheddar

1 tsp chopped fresh parsley

½ tsp chopped fresh thyme

salt and freshly ground black pepper

8 broccoli florets, blanched and halved (see Tip below)

baked potato, to serve

green salad, to serve

1. Heat a non-stick, ovenproof frying pan over a high heat. Add some oil and the leeks, reduce the heat to low and cook for 5 minutes, until soft. Using a slotted spoon, lift the leeks from the pan and set aside. Discard the remaining oil and fry off the bacon. Remove the bacon from the pan with a slotted spoon and drain on kitchen paper.
2. Mix together the eggs, sundried tomatoes, cheddar cheese, parsley, thyme and some salt and pepper in a bowl. Gently stir in the leeks, bacon and broccoli, until coated.
3. Wipe out the pan with kitchen paper. Add about 3 tbsp oil and heat. Add the egg mixture to the pan and cook over a very low heat until the egg begins to set. To prevent the tortilla from sticking, use a spatula to lift it up and allow the uncooked egg to run underneath.
4. Preheat the grill. Place the tortilla under the grill and continue to cook until it's set and golden in colour. This should take about 5 minutes. Keep an eye on it, as the grill can get very hot.
5. To remove the tortilla from the pan, place a plate over the frying pan and invert it. The tortilla should just pop onto the plate. Cut into wedges and serve immediately with a baked potato and green salad.

To blanch the broccoli, bring a large saucepan of water to the boil. Add the broccoli and boil for 2-3 minutes. Remove the broccoli, plunge it into cold water and drain. Or instead of broccoli and to save time, use 1 courgette sliced very thinly, as you won't have to blanch it.

Turkey Koftas with a Korma Sauce

Don't be surprised when you see the amount of ingredients in this recipe – there tends to be a lot in Indian dishes, but they are generally store cupboard ingredients and this dish is fast to make. I always triple the korma sauce recipe, freeze it and make a fish or chicken korma the following week.

Serves 4

For the koftas:

sunflower oil

1 onion, finely chopped

1 garlic clove, finely chopped

2cm fresh ginger, grated

½ tsp ground cumin

½ tsp garam masala

½ tsp turmeric

1 tbsp roughly chopped fresh coriander leaves

600g minced turkey breast

salt and freshly ground black pepper

For the korma sauce:

sunflower oil

1 onion, finely chopped

2 garlic cloves, crushed

½ tsp ground cumin

½ tsp ground coriander

½ tsp turmeric

pinch of garam masala

300ml chicken stock

2 tsp tomato purée

100ml coconut milk

3 tbsp ground almonds

salt and freshly ground black pepper

basmati rice and naan bread, to serve

1. To prepare the koftas, heat a frying pan over a high heat. Add some sunflower oil and the onion, reduce the heat to low and sauté the onion for 7–8 minutes, until softened, taking care not to let it brown. Add the garlic, ginger, cumin, garam masala and turmeric and cook for a further 2 minutes, stirring frequently. Add in the chopped coriander and cook for 1 minute more. Remove from the heat and allow to cool.

2. Place the minced turkey and the onion mixture in a bowl with a little salt and pepper and combine (see the Tip on p. 151). Dampen your hands slightly and shape 1 tablespoon of the mixture into a cylinder. Repeat with the rest of the mixture.

3. Heat some oil in a frying pan over a medium heat and brown the koftas in batches. Lower the heat slightly and cook for a further 10 minutes, or until cooked through. Transfer to a plate and keep warm while the sauce is being prepared.

4. To make the sauce, heat a saucepan over a high heat. Add some oil and the onion, reduce the heat to low and cook for 8–10 minutes, until softened. Add the garlic and cook for a further 2 minutes. Stir in the cumin, coriander, turmeric, garam masala, stock and tomato purée and simmer for 4–5 minutes. Pour in the coconut milk, stir in the ground almonds and simmer for a further 6–7 minutes. Season with salt and pepper to taste.

5. Return the koftas to the pan and heat through. Serve with basmati rice and naan bread.

The koftas are also delicious skewered and cooked on the barbecue.
Serve the korma sauce separately for dipping.

67

Cod Fingers with Mushy Peas and Roasted Sweet Potatoes

This is comfort food for kids ... but I bet you'll have difficulty keeping the adults away. It's surprisingly quick and easy to make your own fish fingers – or goujons if you want to be posh!

Serves 4

For the cod fingers:

150g breadcrumbs

3 tbsp grated Parmesan

1 tbsp chopped fresh parsley

salt and freshly ground black pepper

1 egg, beaten

700g skinless cod, cut into 2cm strips

sunflower oil

For the mushy peas:

150g frozen peas

2 tbsp water

3 tbsp cream

1 small sprig of mint, chopped

salt and freshly ground black pepper

For the sweet potatoes:

500g sweet potatoes, halved and cut into 1cm slices

extra virgin olive oil

salt and freshly ground black pepper

lemon wedges, to serve

1. Preheat the oven to 200°C/fan 180°C/gas 6.
2. To prepare the sweet potatoes, place the slices in a roasting pan, drizzle with oil, salt and pepper and roast for about 20 minutes, until tender. Keep warm.
3. To prepare the cod fingers, combine the breadcrumbs, Parmesan and parsley on a wide plate. Add salt and pepper to taste. Place the beaten egg on a separate wide plate.
4. Dip the fish into the beaten egg, then into the breadcrumb mixture, gently shaking off any excess breadcrumbs. Set the breaded fingers aside on a plate. Repeat the process with the rest of the fish. Place the plate in the fridge for 10 minutes.
5. Meanwhile, to make the mushy peas, put the peas and water in a saucepan and cook for 5–6 minutes, until softened. Roughly mash the peas and add the cream, mint and salt and pepper to taste. Keep warm.
6. Heat some oil in a large frying pan over a medium heat. Add the fish to the pan in batches, taking care not to overcrowd the pan. Fry each side for 2–3 minutes, or until cooked through.
7. To serve, place the mushy peas in a bowl in the centre of a large platter. Pile the cod fingers around the bowl, followed by the roasted sweet potatoes. Serve immediately with lemon wedges.

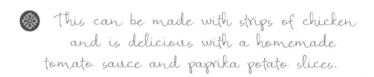 This can be made with strips of chicken and is delicious with a homemade tomato sauce and paprika potato slices.

Quick Pizza

As with all pizza recipes, this can be dressed up a lot more – for example, I sometimes simply spread cream cheese mixed with a dash of wasabi or horseradish over the tortillas, lay smoked trout on top and bake. Finish with capers and lemon zest. This recipe makes a tasty, simple pizza that will keep all the family happy.

Serves 4

extra virgin olive oil

4 flour tortillas

4 tbsp tomato sauce

150g grated mozzarella

12 slices of salami

½ jar of roasted peppers

salt and freshly ground black pepper

1. Preheat the oven to 220°C/fan 200°C/gas 7.
2. Brush a little oil on the top of each tortilla with a pastry brush. Place them on baking sheets, then spread the tomato sauce over the 4 tortillas, leaving a gap of 2cm around the edge. Sprinkle over the mozzarella. Place the salami and roast peppers on top, season to taste with salt and pepper and bake for about 5 minutes, or until the cheese has melted. Serve immediately.

Tortilla wraps can be frozen, so this is a great standby recipe.

Sausage and Sweet Potato Bake

Bangers and mash with onion gravy is an all-time classic. This is my take on this recipe and it's a one-pot dinner, perfect for busy households!

Serves 4

extra virgin olive oil

8 good-quality pork sausages

2 onions, thinly sliced

1 tsp chopped fresh sage

2 garlic cloves, thinly sliced

200g parsnips, thinly sliced (about 3 medium parsnips)

300g sweet potatoes, thinly sliced (about 2 large sweet potatoes)

300ml chicken stock

200ml cream

100ml apple juice

2 tsp wholegrain mustard

salt and freshly ground black pepper

50g Parmesan, grated

1. Preheat the oven to 180°C/fan 160°C/gas 4.
2. Heat some oil in a medium-sized casserole dish over a medium heat. Add the sausages and brown. Remove from the dish, set aside and cut in half lengthwise.
3. Add the onions and sage and sauté for 7–8 minutes on a low heat. Add the garlic and cook for 1 minute more. Remove from the dish and set aside.
4. Place a layer of the parsnips in the casserole dish, followed by the sausages, onions and garlic mix and then sweet potatoes. Continue with a second layer, ending with the sweet potato.
5. Combine the chicken stock, cream, apple juice and mustard, season with salt and pepper and pour over the layers. Top with the grated Parmesan.
6. Place in the oven and bake for 20–25 minutes, or until golden and the vegetable layers are cooked through. From time to time, press the top down with a fish slice to ensure the top layer cooks in the liquid.

Try this dish with sliced celeriac and fennel sausages.

Aromatic Chicken Pilaf

For a casual supper with friends or family, this recipe is always a winner, and not all recipes can be converted to a vegetarian option as easily as this one. Simply replace the chicken with cauliflower florets, peppers, sweetcorn – your favourite vegetables, basically – and cook in the stock with the rice.

Serves 4

sunflower oil

salt and freshly ground black pepper

8 boneless, skinless chicken thighs, cut in half

3 onions, finely sliced

2 garlic cloves, sliced

2 tsp curry powder

100ml white wine

200g basmati rice

500ml chicken stock

100g French beans, sliced

2 tbsp whole almonds, toasted

1 tbsp chopped fresh parsley

1. Heat some oil in a large saucepan over a medium heat. Season the chicken pieces and brown on both sides. Remove and set aside.
2. Add the onion and cook over a low to medium heat for about 10 minutes, until softened and lightly browned. Remove 2 tbsp of the onions and set aside for garnish later. Stir in the garlic and curry powder and cook for a further 2 minutes, adding more oil if necessary.
3. Add the wine and simmer for 2 minutes, then add the rice and stock. Return the chicken to the pan and cover. Bring to the boil, then reduce the heat and simmer for 15–20 minutes, until the chicken is cooked through and all the liquid has been absorbed.
4. Add in the French beans during the last 5 minutes of the cooking time. Scatter over the almonds, reserved onion and parsley. Serve immediately.

For a North African influence, add chickpeas, chopped apricots, lemon zest and toasted pine nuts.

Vietnamese Beef Salad with a Ginger and Lime Dressing

This recipe is known as Bo Luc Lac, which means jumping beef. The beef hops in the pan as it sautés because of the wonderful marinade. But be careful – the marinade often splatters in the hot pan, so stand back! It's a popular recipe in our cookery school and is perfect for a quick lunch or supper. There's no oil in the salad dressing, so it's super healthy too.

Serves 6

For the beef:

2 garlic cloves, minced

2 tbsp oyster sauce

2 tbsp soy sauce

1 tbsp medium-dry sherry

2 x 250g beef fillets, cut into 2cm strips

sunflower oil

For the salad dressing:

2 garlic cloves, minced

1 lime, juice only

½ red chilli, minced

3 tbsp Thai fish sauce (*nam pla*)

2 tbsp sugar

2 tbsp water

1 tbsp freshly grated root ginger

For the salad:

mixed salad leaves

18 cherry tomatoes, halved

½ cucumber, thinly sliced

½ fresh pineapple, cubed

1. To make the marinade, mix the garlic, oyster sauce, soy sauce and sherry together in a bowl. Add the beef and stir to make sure it's coated with the marinade. Refrigerate and leave to marinate for as long as you can but at least 30 minutes.
2. Meanwhile, to prepare the salad, wash the leaves and tear into bite-size pieces. Place in a bowl and add the tomatoes, cucumber and pineapple.
3. Whisk all the salad dressing ingredients together in a jug or place in a sealed jar and shake to emulsify. Set aside.
4. To finish, heat a frying pan over a high heat. Add some oil and heat until it's just smoking. Add the beef, in batches if necessary, taking care not to overcrowd the pan. Sear quickly on full heat on one side and turn over when it's brown. The beef should still be pink in the centre (or to taste). When the beef is ready, remove it from the pan immediately and set aside.
5. Mix half of the dressing with the salad. Divide the salad between 6 plates. Arrange the beef so that it's resting on the salad. Drizzle some of the remaining dressing around the plate with a teaspoon.

Try this with fillet of pork and add some toasted cashew nuts for a crunchy finish to the salad. Replace the pineapple with mango for a delicious change.

78

Thai Red Curry

Here's a very non-Thai idea – a guest at our cookery school told me that a good splash of sherry in a curry just before serving gives a wonderful rounded taste. And you know what? It works!

Serves 4

vegetable oil

3 tbsp red curry paste

275ml coconut milk

100ml chicken stock

200g butternut squash,
peeled and cubed
(about ½ medium squash)

1 large potato, peeled
and cubed

3 chicken breasts, cubed

75g green beans,
quartered

8 cherry tomatoes

6 mushrooms, halved

Thai fish sauce (*nam pla*),
to taste

fresh coriander leaves,
to garnish

jasmine rice, to serve

1. Heat 1 tbsp oil in a large saucepan over a medium heat and fry the curry paste for 1 minute, until fragrant. Add the coconut milk and chicken stock and stir well. Simmer gently for 2 minutes.

2. Add the butternut squash and potato, cover and cook for about 10 minutes, until the vegetables are almost tender. Add the chicken with a little extra stock, if needed, and simmer for 5–7 minutes.

3. Add the rest of the vegetables and simmer for 5 minutes, until they are cooked through. Season with fish sauce to taste.

4. Sprinkle the coriander over and serve with steamed jasmine rice.

 Add a squeeze of lime juice to heighten the curry flavour.

Roast Haddock with Feta and Tomato

To say this dish merely involves assembly is an understatement. There are times when I really appreciate a quick, tasty and colourful dish. All friends and family will enjoy this. Try it with sea bass too – it's delicious.

Serves 4

4 x 200g haddock fillets

extra virgin olive oil

4 tbsp white wine

1 orange, zest and juice

salt and freshly ground black pepper

1 tsp dried oregano

1 x 175g jar of roasted red peppers

120g feta

12 black olives, sliced

4 sprigs of cherry tomatoes on the vine

baked potato, to serve

green salad or steamed green beans, to serve

1. Preheat the oven to 180°C/fan 160°C/gas 4.
2. Place the haddock fillets in an oiled roasting dish. Pour over the white wine and orange juice. Season the fish with a little salt and pepper and sprinkle the orange zest and oregano over. Top with the roasted red peppers, followed by the feta and black olives. Place the sprigs of tomatoes on top.
3. Roast in the oven for 10–12 minutes, or until the fish is cooked through.
4. Serve immediately with a baked potato and a green salad or steamed green beans.

For a Sicilian twist, sit the fish on fennel shavings.

Meat and Fish

Five Flavours
for Meat and Fish

Sometimes meat and fish need a little extra love in the form of interesting flavours and here is some inspiration. It's also a great way to use up leftover spices and mustards – the half jars that are sitting in the larder or fridge taking up space.

1 Mustard Spread

1 lemon, zest and juice

4 tbsp Dijon mustard

2 tbsp horseradish sauce

2 tbsp sunflower oil

2 tbsp chopped fresh parsley

pinch of salt

1. Combine all the ingredients and spread on chicken, beef, pork, lamb or fish before sautéing or roasting.

2 Tandoori Rub

1 tbsp ground ginger

1 tbsp ground cumin

1 tbsp ground coriander

1 tbsp paprika

1 tsp turmeric

1 tsp cayenne

1 tsp salt

1 tsp freshly ground black pepper

1. Combine all the spices. Rub onto lamb, chicken, pork or fish and leave for about 1 hour for the flavours to infuse. Mix the rub with some natural yoghurt to make a tandoori marinade, or simply rub over a leg of lamb or whole chicken before roasting.

3 Teriyaki Marinade

8 tbsp soy sauce

4 tbsp brown sugar

2 tbsp sherry

3 garlic cloves, finely chopped

2 tsp minced ginger

1. Blend all the ingredients together. Use as a marinade for pork, beef, duck, salmon or chicken.

4 Sumac Rub

2 garlic cloves, chopped

1 lemon, zest only

1 orange, zest only

2 tbsp chopped fresh parsley

2 tsp sumac

¼ tsp salt

¼ tsp freshly ground black pepper

1. Blend all the ingredients together in a pestle and mortar. Use as a rub for beef, pork, duck, fish or chicken.

5 Watercress Marinade

1 lemon, zest only

200ml natural yoghurt

80g watercress, stalks included

3 sprigs of fresh mint (optional)

¼ tsp salt

¼ tsp freshly ground black pepper

1. Place all the ingredients in a blender and whizz until smooth. This is a great marinade for fish, chicken and lamb and is also lovely stirred into mashed potato.

Massaman Chicken Curry

This is a rich, creamy, sweet and sour combination that I just love. I make my own curry paste and store it in a jar in the fridge for a few weeks, but when life is too hectic just use a ready-made massaman curry paste.

Serves 6

1.2kg chicken, diced

salt and freshly ground black pepper

sunflower oil

2 onions, sliced

300ml coconut milk

2 tbsp massaman curry paste

4 medium potatoes, peeled and diced

300ml chicken stock

3 cardamom pods, crushed

2 bay leaves

1 cinnamon stick

3 tbsp roasted peanuts

2 tsp brown sugar

2 tsp Thai fish sauce (*nam pla*)

1 tsp tamarind paste

steamed rice, to serve

fresh coriander leaves, to garnish

1. Season the chicken lightly with salt and pepper. Heat some oil in a frying pan and brown the chicken pieces in batches over a high heat. Remove from the pan along with the juices and place in a saucepan.
2. Add a little more oil to the pan, reduce the heat to low and add the onions. Sauté on a low heat for 8–10 minutes, until soft. Remove and add to the chicken.
3. Add 3 tbsp coconut milk to the frying pan and cook for about 20 seconds before adding the curry paste. Cook for 1–2 minutes, until aromatic, then add to the chicken, ensuring all the paste is scraped out of the pan.
4. Add the remaining coconut milk, potatoes, stock, cardamom, bay leaves, cinnamon stick, peanuts, brown sugar, fish sauce and tamarind paste to the chicken. Stir to combine. Place the saucepan on the hob, cover and simmer for about 20 minutes, stirring from time to time, until the chicken and potatoes are tender. Serve with steamed rice and garnish with fresh coriander.

To impress your friends, add 200g prawns to this recipe. Delicious!

Asian Roast Chicken

Roast chicken is always popular, but to have an edge, try these Asian flavours. If you have time, prepare ahead in order for the flavours to develop more.

Serves 4

2 garlic cloves, roughly chopped

2 red chillies, deseeded and roughly chopped

2.5cm fresh root ginger, grated

150g creamed coconut

2 tbsp chopped fresh coriander

1 tsp ground cumin

1 tsp ground coriander

1 tsp turmeric

½ tsp salt

1 x 1.5kg chicken

Stir-fried Green Beans, to serve (see p. 125)

1. Preheat the oven to 190°C/fan 170°C/gas 5.
2. In a small food processor, mix together the garlic, chillies, ginger, creamed coconut, fresh coriander, cumin, ground coriander, turmeric and salt.
3. Place the chicken in an oiled roasting tray. Gently work your hands in under the skin at the crown to separate the skin from the breasts. Spread most of the paste in between the flesh and the skin. Smooth the skin flat with your hand and spread the remaining paste over the legs.
4. Roast for approximately 1 hour 20 minutes, basting the chicken from time to time, until the chicken is fully cooked. Check by inserting a skewer into the thickest part of the leg where it meets the breast. If the juices run clear, the chicken is cooked.

Use the leftovers in a chicken salad with roasted vegetables, rocket and bean sprouts.

Sticky Chicken with Cucumber, Radish and Carrot Pickle

This is a fun dish for entertaining and children will love it too – I make it for the kids' birthday parties. The chicken and pickled vegetables are wrapped up in lettuce leaves and eaten with your hands.

Serves 4

For the chicken:

2 garlic cloves, minced

3 tbsp sugar

1 ½ tbsp Thai fish sauce (*nam pla*)

1 ½ tbsp sunflower oil

1 tbsp fresh lime juice

1 ½ tsp hot chilli sauce

800g chicken breasts, cut crosswise into 0.5cm-thick slices

For the pickle:

6 radishes

3 medium carrots, peeled

1 cucumber

220ml rice vinegar

100g sugar

2 tsp salt

To serve:

crisp iceberg lettuce leaves

2 tbsp alfalfa sprouts (optional)

1. To marinate the chicken, whisk together the garlic, sugar, fish sauce, oil, lime juice and chilli sauce in a large bowl until the sugar is dissolved. Add the chicken and toss to coat. Refrigerate for about 2 hours.
2. To make the pickle, julienne the radishes, carrots and cucumber (i.e. cut into very thin strips). Whisk together the vinegar, sugar and salt in a bowl until the sugar is dissolved. Add the vegetables and toss to combine. Leave to stand for about 30 minutes, until the vegetables are wilted.
3. To cook the chicken, heat a griddle pan over a medium heat. Cook the chicken in batches, taking care not to overcrowd the pan. Allow to colour on one side before turning over to brown on the other side, which should take 3–4 minutes, depending on the thickness of the chicken. This will give a lovely caramel flavour. When the chicken is fully cooked, transfer to a warmed serving plate.
4. Strain the pickled vegetables and arrange around the chicken. To serve, place a lettuce leaf on your plate and top with the pickled vegetables, alfalfa sprouts and chicken. Fold over the lettuce and enjoy.

 Rice wine vinegar has a lower acidic level, so if you can't get rice wine vinegar from your local Asian shop, use white wine vinegar and add 1 tbsp water to dilute it.

Tequila Chicken

A hearty dish, this falls under the winter warmer category and is wonderful for casual entertaining.

Serves 4

75g raisins

7 tbsp tequila, divided

1 x 1.5kg chicken, skin on and jointed (ask your butcher to do this)

100g seasoned flour

extra virgin olive oil

2 shallots, thinly sliced

2 garlic cloves, crushed

1 Granny Smith apple, peeled, cored and diced

100g flaked almonds

500ml chicken stock

salt and freshly ground black pepper

2 tbsp chopped fresh flat-leaf parsley

wild rice, to serve

1. Soak the raisins in 3 tbsp tequila for 20 minutes.
2. Meanwhile, dredge the chicken pieces in the seasoned flour, shaking off any excess flour. Heat some oil in a large casserole dish and gently brown the chicken in batches. Set aside.
3. Add a little more oil to the casserole dish and sauté the shallots over a low heat for about 5 minutes. Add the garlic and cook for a further 2 minutes.
4. Add the diced apple to the onions, along with the almonds and soaked raisins, including the tequila they were soaked in.
5. Return the chicken to the casserole dish and pour in the stock and the remaining 4 tbsp tequila. Cover and bring to the boil, then reduce to a simmer for about 30 minutes, or until the chicken is cooked through. Check for seasoning, adding salt and pepper as required. Sprinkle with chopped parsley and serve with wild rice.

Use the leftovers, if any, shredded with a salad in pittas.

Pork Chop Parcels

When I make these for the children, I usually omit the dill – they don't seem to appreciate it! But everyone loves pork chops. These are also lovely pan-fried for supper after a busy day at work.

Serves 4

4 x 150g pork chops (ask your butcher to trim them)

salt and freshly ground black pepper

extra virgin olive oil

120ml cider or unsweetened apple juice

4 tbsp crème fraîche

For the stuffing:

extra virgin olive oil

3 shallots, finely chopped

2 celery stalks, finely chopped

1 garlic clove, finely chopped

30g butter, melted

100g fresh breadcrumbs

4 tbsp finely chopped dried apricots

2 tbsp chopped fresh dill

2 tbsp chopped fresh parsley

1 tbsp chopped fresh mint

salt and freshly ground black pepper

To serve:

sweet potato mash

wilted spinach

1. To prepare the stuffing, heat a saucepan over a high heat. Add some oil and the shallots and celery, reduce the heat to low and sauté for 5–6 minutes, until softened. Add the garlic and sauté for 1 minute more.
2. Add the butter and allow to melt. Add the breadcrumbs, apricots, dill, parsley and mint. Season with salt and pepper to taste. Mix well, remove from the heat and allow to cool.
3. Using a sharp knife, make an incision or 'pocket' in each chop. Season the pork on both sides. Stuff the chop with the cooled stuffing.
4. Heat some oil in a frying pan over a high heat and sauté the chops until they are browned. Pour in the cider or apple juice, reduce the heat to low, cover the pan and continue to cook for 7–8 minutes, depending on the thickness of the chops, until the juices run clear. Stir in the crème fraîche.
5. Serve the chops with the pan juices spooned over and with a sweet potato mash and wilted spinach.

This stuffing is delicious with chicken breasts too.

Roast Breast of Duck with Spiced Plums

This is a marvellous recipe for when friends are visiting. Everybody loves duck, so here's a twist on the usual recipe. We have an abundance of plums in our garden in early autumn, but this is also delicious with apricots.

Serves 4

4 x 170g duck breasts, skin on

1 tsp ground cumin

salt and freshly ground black pepper

sunflower oil

1 garlic clove, finely chopped

2cm fresh root ginger, grated

3 oranges (juice of 3 oranges and zest of 1 orange)

100ml chicken stock

2 star anise

4 tbsp honey

1 tbsp soy sauce

½ tsp ground coriander

4 plums, stoned and quartered

egg noodles with a dash of soy sauce, to serve

orange zest thinly sliced into strips, to garnish

1. Score each duck breast with a sharp knife and rub with the cumin, salt and pepper. Heat some oil in a heavy-based frying pan over a high heat and fry the duck, skin side down first, for 3 minutes. Turn over, reduce the heat and cook for about 7 minutes more, until tender. Remove from the pan and keep warm.

2. To make the sauce, retain the duck fat in the pan, adding more oil if necessary. Gently cook the garlic and ginger until slightly golden, about 1 minute. Add the orange zest and juice, stock, star anise, honey, soy sauce and ground coriander. Bring to the boil and allow to reduce for 4–5 minutes. Add in the plums and simmer for a further 3 minutes. Add salt and pepper to taste.

3. Place the soy noodles on a platter. Slice the duck breasts and place on top of the noodles. Scatter over the orange zest. Spoon the sauce over the duck breasts and serve.

 *Try this with pork chops.*

Sesame Pork Meatballs with Pappardelle

The Italian side of my family might well tut tut for suggesting pappardelle with Asian-influenced meatballs, but they're a cracking good combination.

Serves 4

For the pork meatballs:

500g lean minced pork

4 spring onions, finely chopped

2 garlic cloves, chopped

100g fresh breadcrumbs

30g sesame seeds, toasted

3 tbsp oyster sauce

2 tsp wholegrain mustard

1 egg, beaten

salt and freshly ground black pepper

sunflower oil

For the pappardelle:

300g pappardelle

3 tbsp butter

2 tbsp sweet chilli sauce

1 tsp sesame oil

1. Combine the pork mince, spring onions, garlic, breadcrumbs, sesame seeds, oyster sauce, mustard, beaten egg and salt and pepper in a bowl and mix well. Fry a tiny piece of the mixture and check for seasoning, adjusting the main mixture if required.
2. Using wet hands, roll the mixture into 20 meatballs.
3. Put a large pot of water on to boil for the pasta.
4. Heat a frying pan over a medium heat. Add some oil and sauté the meatballs for about 10 minutes, until cooked through.
5. Meanwhile, cook the pappardelle according to the instructions on the packet. Drain and toss with the butter, sweet chilli sauce and sesame oil.
6. Divide the pasta immediately between 4 plates and place the meatballs on top.

 These meatballs are lovely served on cocktail sticks as finger food.

Minty Lamb Casserole

Being lamb farmers here at Ballyknocken, we are always looking for new ideas to use all cuts of lamb. Neck of lamb works well here too, making it even more economical.

Serves 4

extra virgin olive oil

800g shoulder of lamb, trimmed and diced

salt and freshly ground black pepper

3 carrots, peeled and chopped

3 parsnips, peeled and chopped

2 onions, chopped

2 garlic cloves, chopped

2 tbsp flour

2 lemons, zest only

150ml white wine

1 litre lamb or chicken stock

500g Charlotte (baby) potatoes, washed and left whole

2 tbsp chopped fresh mint

150g frozen peas

1. Preheat the oven to 180°C /fan 160°C/gas 4.
2. Heat some oil in a large casserole dish. Season the lamb and brown in batches on all sides, taking care not to overcrowd the dish. Remove and set aside.
3. Add more oil to the casserole dish if necessary, followed by the carrots, parsnips, onions and garlic. Sauté for about 10 minutes, until the onions are soft. Add the flour and lemon zest and cook for about 1 minute, then gradually add the white wine and cook for a further 1 minute. Pour in the stock, bring to the boil and reduce to a simmer.
4. Return the lamb to the casserole, along with the potatoes and mint. Cover with a lid and place in the oven for 1 ½ hours, or until the potatoes are cooked and the meat is tender. Add the peas for the remaining 10 minutes of cooking time.
5. Just before serving, skim the fat off the top with a ladle and check for seasoning, adding more salt and pepper as required.

To sweeten this dish, consider adding 50g of chopped dried apricots.

Moroccan Lamb with Dates and Almonds

Lamb and couscous is a marriage made in heaven. The trick is to flavour the couscous appropriately. I add lemon zest and juice, apricots, fresh coriander, toasted almonds and extra virgin olive oil to mine. The leftovers are wonderful as a salad the following day.

Serves 4

1 tsp ground cinnamon

1 tsp ground cumin

1 tsp ground coriander

pinch of saffron

2 tsp water

4 leg of lamb steaks, trimmed

salt and freshly ground black pepper

extra virgin olive oil

1 onion, finely chopped

1 ½ tbsp tomato purée

400ml chicken stock

1 x 400g tin of chickpeas, drained and rinsed

12 pitted dates

4 tbsp blanched whole almonds, toasted

2 tbsp chopped fresh coriander

couscous, to serve

1. Place the cinnamon, cumin, coriander, saffron and water in a large bowl. Add the lamb steaks, coat well and leave to marinate for at least 1 hour.
2. Heat some oil in a large casserole over a medium heat. Season the lamb and sauté the steaks until nicely browned on both sides. You will need to do this in batches so as not to overcrowd the dish. Remove the lamb and set aside.
3. Add more oil to the casserole, reduce the heat to low and sauté the onion for approximately 7 minutes, until golden brown. Add the tomato purée and chicken stock and bring to the boil.
4. Return the lamb to the casserole. Cover, reduce the heat and simmer for about 40 minutes. Stir in the chickpeas and dates and cook for a further 15 minutes. Check that the lamb is tender and cooked through, then add the almonds, reserving a few for the garnish. Add salt and pepper to taste. Sprinkle the chopped coriander and almonds over the top and serve with couscous.

Chicken is delicious in this recipe instead of the lamb and it cooks a lot faster.

Mustard and Herb Lamb Cutlets with Honey Dressing

I made this recently for visitors from NBC's Today Show to much applause. My dad, the lamb farmer in the family, was delighted, as they pronounced that Wicklow lamb was the best they'd ever tasted.

Serves 4

For the lamb:

200g fresh breadcrumbs

½ lemon, zest only

1 ½ tsp very finely chopped fresh rosemary

3 tbsp seasoned flour

12 lamb cutlets, French trimmed (get your butcher to do this for you)

4 tbsp wholegrain honey mustard

extra virgin olive oil

For the dressing:

4 tbsp wholegrain honey mustard

4 tbsp extra virgin olive oil

1 tbsp clear honey

2 tsp red wine vinegar

salt and freshly ground black pepper

Herby Champ, to serve (see p. 123)

1. To make the dressing, combine the mustard, oil, honey, vinegar and salt and pepper in a bowl. Set aside.

2. To prepare the chops, combine the breadcrumbs, lemon zest and rosemary in a bowl. Place the seasoned flour on a plate. Dip the chops into the flour, shaking off the excess. Spread the honey mustard on both sides of each chop. Finally, dip the chops into the rosemary breadcrumbs, pressing firmly. Allow to set in the fridge for about 30 minutes.

3. Heat some oil in a large frying pan. When hot, sear the lamb chops on both sides to colour, turning carefully to ensure the crumb coating doesn't fall off. Reduce the heat and cook for 3–4 minutes, depending on the thickness of the cutlets, or until the meat is cooked to taste. Remove from the pan, drizzle the dressing over the chops and serve with Herby Champ.

 Redcurrant jelly is an ideal accompaniment for these lamb chops.

Roast Leg of Lamb with Redcurrant Sauce

This recipe was influenced by the fact that our lambs actually ate all my redcurrants last year when they edged their way through the fence into my organic vegetable garden. Our guests joked about redcurrant-infused lamb, hence the idea for this delicious dish. I have also cooked this with raspberries instead of redcurrants.

Serves 4

For the lamb:

3 tbsp extra virgin olive oil

1 tbsp chopped fresh oregano

1 tbsp chopped fresh rosemary

1 tbsp chopped fresh parsley

salt and freshly ground black pepper

1 x 1.5kg leg of lamb

4 garlic cloves, peeled and sliced

20 shallots, peeled and kept whole

150ml red wine

150ml chicken stock

For the redcurrant sauce:

125g redcurrants

4 tbsp redcurrant jelly

2 tbsp brown sugar

1 tbsp chopped fresh rosemary leaves

salt and freshly ground black pepper

1. Preheat the oven to 180°C/fan 160°C/gas 4.
2. Mix the oil, herbs and salt and pepper together. Place the lamb on an oiled roasting tin and rub the olive oil mix over it. Make incisions in the lamb and tuck in the sliced garlic.
3. Place the lamb and shallots in the oven and roast for about 30 minutes. Add the wine and stock and roast for a further 40 minutes, or until the lamb is cooked. Baste from time to time.
4. Remove the meat and shallots from the roasting tin and keep warm. Allow the lamb to rest for 15 minutes. Strain the fat from the tin.
5. To make the sauce, place the roasting tin on the hob over a medium heat and reduce the liquid to taste. Add the redcurrants, redcurrant jelly, sugar and rosemary and simmer for 3 minutes. Check for seasoning, adding salt and pepper to taste.
6. Carve the lamb and serve with the sauce.

Add wild mushrooms to this dish for an autumnal twist.

Pot-roasted Carbonnade of Beef (Slow Cooker)

A slow cooker is a great invention for busy households. Everything can be prepared in the morning and left to cook all day. The beefy, beer aromas will waft throughout the house, greeting you on your return home.

Serve 4

sunflower oil

1.5kg topside beef

salt and freshly ground black pepper

300ml Guinness

300ml beef stock

2 medium onions, finely chopped

2 garlic cloves, chopped

2 medium carrots, peeled and sliced

2 celery stalks, chopped

1 orange, zest only

3 sprigs of thyme

2 bay leaves

3 tbsp redcurrant jelly

2 tbsp water

2 tbsp cornflour

mashed potatoes, to serve

1. Turn the slow cooker on to high for 20 minutes.
2. Meanwhile, heat some oil in a large frying pan over a high heat. Season the beef and brown all over. Remove from the pan and place in the slow cooker. Deglaze the pan with a little of the Guinness and add these juices to the beef.
3. Pour the remaining Guinness and stock over the beef in the slow cooker. Add the onions, garlic, carrots, celery, orange zest, thyme, bay leaves, redcurrant jelly and salt and pepper. Stir well. Put the lid on and cook on low for 8–10 hours.
4. Remove the thyme sprigs and bay leaves and discard. Place the beef on a carving board, cover and keep warm.
5. In a small bowl, add 2 tbsp water to the cornflour and mix until smooth. Stir into the gravy in the slow cooker until it begins to thicken. Check for seasoning, adding salt and pepper as required.
6. Carve the meat in slices, transfer to a serving platter and spoon the gravy over the meat. Serve with the vegetables and fluffy mashed potatoes.

✽ Pan-fry some wild mushrooms with garlic and thyme and add it at the end.

Roast Sirloin of Beef, Oriental Style

Roast beef is the ultimate Sunday roast. For an unusual twist, this recipe gives a slight hint of spice to the beef, and the Celeriac and Potato Mash is a great contrast to the rich flavours in this dish. The sauce can be thickened with cornflour to taste, but I prefer not to as the flavours are so deliciously intense.

Serves 6

vegetable oil

1 x 1.2kg piece of beef sirloin or rib eye

4 shallots, roughly chopped

2 garlic cloves, chopped

5cm fresh root ginger, peeled and cut into thin strips

1 tsp Chinese five spice

200ml beef stock (may require more, to taste)

4 tbsp dark soy sauce

1 tbsp Chinese rice wine or dry sherry

1 tsp sugar

salt and freshly ground black pepper

1 red pepper, sliced

1 yellow pepper, sliced

1. Preheat the oven to 180°C/fan 160°C/gas 4.
2. Heat some oil in a large casserole dish over a high heat. Add the beef and brown on all sides. Remove the beef and set aside.
3. Reduce the heat and add the shallots, garlic, ginger and Chinese five spice to the dish. Fry for 3 minutes, stirring occasionally. Add the beef stock, soy sauce, rice wine, sugar and salt and pepper. Bring to the boil and cook briskly for 5 minutes.
4. Return the beef to the casserole dish, turning it to coat in the cooking liquid. Cover and place in the oven for approximately 50 minutes, or until the beef is cooked to your liking. Add the sliced peppers about 15 minutes before the beef has completed cooking.
5. When the beef is done, remove it from the casserole, cover and leave for 10 minutes to rest before carving. Place the casserole on the hob to keep the sauce warm.
6. Serve the beef sliced on a platter, surrounded by the peppers, and drizzle the sauce over.

 Serve with roasted parsnips and butternut squash for a flavoursome and colourful dinner.

Butternut Squash and Beef Casserole

Butternut squash and beef might not be the first combination that springs to mind, but they do work very well together and are very colourful for presentation.

Serves 4

700g round steak, trimmed and diced

100g seasoned flour

extra virgin olive oil

3 red onions, finely chopped

2 garlic cloves, finely sliced

1 small butternut squash, peeled and diced

1 red pepper, roughly chopped

1 yellow pepper, roughly chopped

2 sprigs of thyme

650ml beef stock

3 tbsp tomato purée

2 tsp balsamic vinegar

salt and freshly ground black pepper

steamed rice or garlic mashed potatoes (see p. 120), to serve

1. Preheat the oven to 180°C/fan 160°C/gas 4.
2. Toss the beef in the seasoned flour in a Ziploc bag and shake the beef until coated. Remove the beef from the bag and shake off the excess flour.
3. Heat some oil in a casserole over a medium heat and add the beef in batches. Brown well on both sides and set aside.
4. Add a little more oil to the casserole. Reduce the heat to low, add the onions and sauté for 8–10 minutes, until the onions are soft. Add the garlic and cook for a further 2 minutes. Add the diced butternut squash, peppers, thyme, stock, tomato purée and balsamic vinegar and return the beef to the casserole.
5. Cook in the oven for 1 ½ hours or until the beef is tender, stirring occasionally. Check for seasoning, adding salt and pepper as required, and serve.

 Prepare this a day or two ahead. As with all casseroles, the flavours improve over time.

Orange and Oregano Cod with Chorizo and New Potatoes

In this recipe, I introduced some sunshine in the form of orange zest and paprika, just to remind you of your favourite Spanish holiday. I've used cod, but any white fish works well.

Serves 4

2 tbsp extra virgin olive oil, plus extra to drizzle

100g chorizo, sliced

600g new potatoes, thinly sliced

2 garlic cloves, chopped

salt and freshly ground black pepper

300ml vegetable stock

100ml dry white wine

1 orange, zest only

2 tsp mild paprika (smoked if possible)

1 tsp dried oregano

4 x 175g fillets of fresh cod

200g cherry tomatoes

2 tbsp chopped fresh flat-leaf parsley

1. Heat the oil in a large casserole dish with a lid and sauté the chorizo over a medium heat for 2 minutes, until it starts to release its oils. Add the sliced potatoes and garlic to the chorizo and season lightly with salt and pepper.
2. Add the stock and wine. Turn down the heat and cook for 15 minutes, until the potatoes are just cooked. Lift the potatoes occasionally with a fish slice to prevent them from sticking.
3. Mix together the orange zest, paprika, oregano and some salt and pepper in a bowl and sprinkle generously over the fish. Place the fish on top of the potatoes, along with the cherry tomatoes and chopped parsley.
4. Cover the casserole dish with a lid and cook for 5–7 minutes, or until the fish is cooked through. Drizzle with olive oil and serve.

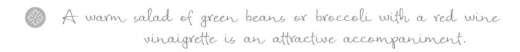 A warm salad of green beans or broccoli with a red wine vinaigrette is an attractive accompaniment.

Seafood and Spinach Open Ravioli

Everybody loves a good fish pie and this is my take on it. It looks really well layering the lasagne sheets with the seafood sauce. Equally, you can use the sauce section of the recipe and place in a casserole with mashed potatoes on top for a quick fish pie.

Serves 4

150g broccoli florets, cut into bite-sized pieces

100g undyed smoked haddock, cut into bite-sized pieces

100g salmon, cut into bite-sized pieces

100g cod, cut into bite-sized pieces

600ml milk

1 bay leaf

100g cooked prawns

30g butter

1 onion, finely chopped

100g sweetcorn

2 tbsp chopped fresh dill

salt and freshly ground black pepper

8 lasagne sheets

4 tbsp grated Parmesan

1 tbsp chopped fresh parsley

For the roux:

100g butter

100g flour

1. Preheat the oven to 180°C/fan 160°C/gas 4.

2. Steam the broccoli until it's just done (al dente). Drain and transfer to a bowl of iced water to cool and to stop the cooking process. Set aside.

3. Ensure there are no bones or skin on the fish (your fishmonger will do this for you). In a large saucepan, poach the haddock, salmon and cod in the milk with the bay leaf. Simmer gently for about 5 minutes, or until the fish is almost cooked (the cooking time will depend on the size of the diced fish). Add the prawns and heat through, which will take about 1 minute. Remove the fish and bay leaf and set aside. Retain the milk in the saucepan and keep it hot (it will be used to make the sauce).

4. Melt the butter in a saucepan. Add the onion and cook gently over a low heat for 10 minutes, or until the onion is soft. Remove from the pan and set aside.

5. To make the roux, melt the butter, then add the flour. Stir constantly for 2–3 minutes, until it forms a ball. Gradually pour the hot milk into the roux, whisking constantly. Use enough of the milk so that the sauce coats the back of a spoon. Add the broccoli, onion, sweetcorn and chopped dill. Season with salt and pepper to taste and heat through. Gently add the fish to the sauce, taking care not to break it. Stir and keep warm.

6. Meanwhile, cook the lasagne sheets according to the packet instructions. Drain and allow to cool slightly, then cut in half width wise.

7. To serve, place a lasagne sheet on each serving plate, spoon over some of the seafood sauce and fish and continue layering, finishing with a lasagna sheet. Sprinkle with Parmesan and parsley and serve.

 I use a scissors to cut my cooked lasagne — works every time!

Baked Haddock Portuguese

The mother of a Portuguese friend of mine gave this recipe to me many years ago. I often make it for the children and they enjoy the Mediterranean flavours of the dish.

Serves 4

extra virgin olive oil

2 garlic cloves, sliced

2 x 400g tins of cherry tomatoes

12 green pitted olives

12 black pitted olives

2 tbsp chopped fresh basil

1 tbsp capers

2 tsp sugar

salt and freshly ground black pepper

300g spinach

4 x 150g fresh haddock fillets

2 lemon slices, cut in half

1 tbsp chopped fresh flat-leaf parsley

1. Preheat the oven to 200°C/fan 180°C/gas 6.
2. Heat some oil in a frying pan over a low heat and gently cook the garlic for 1 minute, stirring frequently. Add the tinned tomatoes, olives, basil, capers, sugar and a little salt and pepper. Cook for 15 minutes, until the sauce has thickened and reduced. Check for seasoning and adjust as required.
3. Pour the sauce into a large roasting dish, such as a lasagne dish. Spread the spinach down the centre and season with salt and pepper. Place the fish on top and arrange half a lemon slice on each fillet. Drizzle with oil and season again with salt and pepper.
4. Transfer to the oven and cook for 12–15 minutes, or until the fish is cooked through. Sprinkle with chopped parsley to serve.

 Baked potatoes with herb butter taste wonderful with this dish.

Salmon with a Gazpacho Salsa

This is a little unusual, as of course the gazpacho is served cold with the hot salmon, but it's really popular in our cookery school. It's no problem to heat the sauce if you prefer. It's a great way to get the kids to eat more veg!

Serves 4

4 x 150g salmon darnes

extra virgin olive oil

4 tbsp pesto

salt and freshly ground black pepper

lemon wedges, to serve

For the gazpacho sauce:

2 tomatoes, skinned, deseeded and diced (see Tip below)

2 shallots, finely diced

1 cucumber, diced

1 red pepper, deseeded and diced

1 garlic clove, finely sliced

150ml passata (sieved tomatoes)

100ml extra virgin olive oil

2 tbsp red wine vinegar

2 tbsp water

1 tbsp chopped fresh flat-leaf parsley

1 tsp chopped fresh chives

salt and freshly ground black pepper

1. Preheat the oven to 180°C/fan 160°C/gas 4. Line a baking tray with parchment paper.

2. To prepare the sauce, combine all the ingredients in a bowl, season with salt and pepper to taste and mix well. Place in the fridge.

3. Brush each salmon darne with oil and spread 1 tbsp pesto on the presentation side of each darne. Place the salmon presentation side up on the lined baking tray. Cook in the oven for 10–15 minutes, or until firm to the touch.

4. To serve, spoon some gazpacho sauce onto the middle of a serving plate. Carefully place a piece of salmon in the centre. Drizzle a little sauce on top. Serve immediately with lemon wedges.

To skin a tomato, remove the hard core at the centre of the tomato with a sharp-pointed knife. Cut a cross at the bottom. Plunge into boiling water for 60 seconds, then into iced water. The skin will just peel off.

Pancetta-wrapped Sea Bass with Asparagus, Lime and Dill Drizzle

When the family come round for a light lunch, this is my reliable crowd pleaser. Couple with a glass of chilled white wine for guaranteed satisfaction.

Serves 4

1 bunch fresh asparagus (about 12 spears), woody ends removed

4 sea bass fillets, boned

salt and freshly ground black pepper

8 pancetta slices (2 per fillet)

extra virgin olive oil

100g crème fraîche

2 tbsp mayonnaise

1 tsp chopped fresh dill

1 lime (zest of 1 and juice of ½)

sprigs of dill, to serve

lime wedges, to serve

1. Preheat the oven to 200°C/fan 180°C/gas 6.
2. Blanch the asparagus in a large saucepan of boiling salted water for 2–3 minutes. Drain and transfer to a bowl of iced water to cool and to stop the cooking process.
3. Season each fish fillet with salt and pepper. Place 3 asparagus spears on top and wrap with 2 slices of pancetta. Brush with oil.
4. Place in an oiled ovenproof baking dish and cook for 6–8 minutes, until the fish is cooked and the pancetta is crisp.
5. Meanwhile, combine the crème fraîche, mayonnaise and dill in a bowl. Stir in the lime zest and juice. Taste, adding salt and pepper if required.
6. Serve the fish fillets on individual plates and spoon over the lime crème fraîche. Garnish with sprigs of dill and lime wedges.

 You can replace the sea bass with trout fillets or salmon.

Vegetable and Potato Sides

Five Ways
with Mash

You can vary the vegetables you use for this recipe by adding celeriac, carrot, parsnip, turnip or using a combination of whatever vegetables you have to hand. But one thing is for sure — never scrimp on the butter and cream or milk and season well with salt and pepper to taste. If you need to keep the mash warm, simply put it in a metal bowl covered with foil and place over a pot of simmering water.

1 Celeriac and Potato

Don't let the appearance of the celeriac put you off. This works well with equal quantities of celeriac and potatoes. Remember to season well with salt and pepper. Add ½ tsp ground cumin when serving the mash with casseroles, such as the Minty Lamb Casserole (see p. 100).

2 Roast Garlic

Incorporating 5 or 6 caramelised roasted cloves of garlic into the mash gives a smooth and flavoursome mash. For extra zing, add 2 tsp paprika.

3 Pesto

For a quick, colourful mash, swirl in 3 tbsp pesto for an Italian twist!

4 Wasabi

If you like sushi, you'll think this combination is awesome. Blend a little wasabi paste into the potatoes – just be careful about how much you use, unless you like it hot!

5 Sweet Potato and Lime

Mash some sweet potatoes and blend with some regular mashed potatoes so that it's half sweet potatoes, half regular potatoes. Add the zest of 1 lime and the juice of ½ lime – and butter and cream of course!

Stir-fried Green Beans

Mangetout or broccoli are also lovely alternatives to the beans in this recipe. A handy time-saving tip is that there is no need to steam the mangetout, they will cook on the wok.

Serves 4

300g green beans

2 tbsp sunflower oil

4 spring onions, sliced

2 garlic cloves, minced

1 red chilli, deseeded and chopped

1 ½ tbsp Thai fish sauce (*nam pla*)

1 tsp sugar

freshly ground black pepper

1. Lightly steam the green beans until they're just cooked (al dente). Drain and transfer to a bowl of iced water to cool and to stop the cooking process. Set aside.
2. Place a wok on a very high heat. Add the oil followed by the spring onions, garlic and chilli. Stir-fry for 2 minutes, taking care that the garlic doesn't burn.
3. Add the green beans and stir-fry for about 1 minute, until heated through, then add the fish sauce, sugar and pepper. Check for seasoning, adding more fish sauce or pepper to taste.

Wok frying is a swift way of adding flavour to hum-drum vegetables. My wok is invaluable to me. To take care of it, I simply wipe it out well every time after use rather than washing it.

Roasted Root Vegetable Gratin

During the autumn, I often serve this as a vegetarian main course and add a few slices of apple when roasting the vegetables. It's also delicious with roasted lamb or pork for the 'where's the meat?' brigade in my family.

Serves 4

200g potatoes, peeled and cut into bite-sized chunks

200g turnips, peeled and cut into bite-sized chunks

200g carrots, peeled and cut into bite-sized chunks

200g celeriac, peeled and cut into bite-sized chunks

200g parsnips, peeled and cut into bite-sized chunks

2 medium onions, sliced

1 garlic clove, crushed

3 tbsp sunflower oil

3 tbsp wholegrain mustard

2 tbsp honey

1 tbsp chopped fresh parsley

1 tbsp chopped fresh rosemary

salt and freshly ground black pepper

100ml cream

For the topping:

120g fresh breadcrumbs

70g hazelnuts, toasted and chopped

60g butter, melted

4 tbsp grated Gruyère cheese

salt and freshly ground black pepper

1. Preheat the oven to 200°C/fan 180°C/gas 6.
2. Combine the potatoes, turnips, carrots, celeriac, parsnips, onions and garlic in a large roasting dish.
3. Whisk together the oil, mustard and honey and pour over the vegetables. Mix well. Sprinkle the parsley and rosemary over the top. Season with salt and pepper.
4. Cover with tin foil and roast for about 50 minutes. Remove the foil cover, add the cream and stir well.
5. Mix all the ingredients for the topping together in a bowl and sprinkle over the roasted vegetables. Return to the oven for 20 minutes, until golden brown.

❁ Add 2 tsp harissa paste to the vegetables when roasting for a more Moroccan/Tunisian flavour.

Creamy Curly Kale

I have an abundance of curly kale in our garden here at Ballyknocken. My favourite is the purple curly kale, but watch out, you might have pink fingers after handling it!

Serves 4

30g butter

2 tbsp extra virgin olive oil

4 shallots, finely sliced

2 garlic cloves, chopped

3 tbsp sour cream

2 tbsp cream

salt and freshly ground black pepper

250g curly kale, washed and roughly chopped

1. Melt the butter and oil in a frying pan. Add the shallots and sauté on a low heat for about 5 minutes, until golden and soft. Add the garlic and cook for a further 1–2 minutes. Add the sour cream, cream and salt and pepper to taste and heat through.
2. Place the curly kale in a saucepan. Cover the kale with boiling water and add a pinch of salt. Cover with a lid and wilt for about 3–4 minutes. Drain well.
3. Place the kale in a serving dish and drizzle the cream mixture on top.

This recipe is equally good with spinach.

Cheesy Courgette Bake

This is a great way to use up a surplus of courgettes as well as getting the children to eat more vegetables. I often add a few tablespoons of peas or even sweetcorn.

Serves 4

extra virgin olive oil

8 spring onions, chopped

4 medium courgettes, diced

3 large eggs

160g grated cheddar

2 tbsp wholegrain mustard

salt and freshly ground black pepper

80g breadcrumbs

4 tbsp chopped fresh parsley

1. Preheat the oven to 200°C/fan 180°C/gas 6. Butter a large, shallow dish.
2. Heat a large frying pan over a medium heat and add some oil. Lightly sauté the spring onions and courgettes. When barely softened, remove the vegetables with a slotted spoon and discard any excess liquid. Place the spring onions and courgettes in the buttered ovenproof dish.
3. Whisk the eggs with the cheddar, mustard and salt and pepper in a bowl. Pour the cheese and egg mixture over the courgettes and spring onions, then sprinkle with the breadcrumbs and parsley. Bake for 15 minutes, until golden.

To make a full one-pot meal from this recipe, place some white fish fillets at the base of the ovenproof dish, pour over the courgette mixture and bake as per the recipe.

BBQs, Salads and Picnics

Five Quick
Salad Dressings

Salad dressing is designed to enhance the vegetables, so a really good salad dressing is vital. Here are some of my favourites. They are very easy to make – I put the ingredients in an old jam jar, seal the lid and shake to emulsify. Generally, dressings will keep for about 1 week in the fridge.

1 Ballyknocken House Salad Dressing

6 tbsp extra virgin olive oil

2 tbsp red wine vinegar

1 tsp local honey

1 tsp wholegrain mustard

salt and freshly ground black pepper

2 Herb Dressing

Using the above recipe, add 2 tbsp freshly chopped herbs, such as chives, marjoram, parsley and some thyme.

3 Wasabi Dressing

Using the recipe on p. 133, add a little wasabi (¼ tsp) to the dressing instead of the mustard. Don't be too heavy handed with the wasabi!

4 Sweet Orange and Basil Dressing

Using the recipe on p. 133, add the juice and zest of 1 orange and 2 tbsp shredded fresh basil.

5 Chilli Dressing

Using the recipe on p. 133, add 1 tbsp chilli sauce instead of the mustard and add ½ red chilli (optional), chopped.

Oriental Salad

I'm always looking for tasty side dishes to accompany rich Asian-style main courses and this salad, with its zingy dressing, hits the mark.

Serves 4

For the salad:

sunflower oil

2 tbsp chopped unsalted peanuts

¼ head Chinese cabbage or ¼ head iceberg lettuce, shredded

3 spring onions, sliced

1 red onion, thinly sliced

100g grated carrot

100g bean sprouts

2 tbsp chopped fresh mint

a small bunch of fresh coriander, chopped

For the salad dressing:

1 red chilli, deseeded and chopped

1 large garlic clove, crushed

1 lime, juice only

6 tbsp sunflower oil

1 tbsp brown sugar

2 tsp rice vinegar

2 tsp Thai fish sauce (*nam pla*)

1. To prepare the salad, heat some oil in a frying pan and fry the peanuts until golden. Remove and drain on kitchen paper.
2. To make the dressing, place all the ingredients in a jug and whisk to combine. Check for seasoning and adjust to taste with extra Thai fish sauce or lime juice.
3. Mix the Chinese cabbage or iceberg lettuce with the spring onions, red onion, carrots, bean sprouts, mint, coriander and enough dressing to coat. Sprinkle with the peanuts and serve.

 This is delicious with the Thai-style Crab Cakes (see p. 15).

BLT Salad

The whole family loves this one and it's part of the school lunchbox on a regular basis. My daughter especially likes salads, but my son is still getting used to anything green!

Serves 4

For the salad:

⅓ baguette

extra virgin olive oil

1 garlic clove, peeled and halved

salt and freshly ground black pepper

1 head radicchio, leaves separated and torn

½ head iceberg lettuce, leaves separated and torn

16 cherry tomatoes, halved

3 sundried tomatoes, finely chopped

8 slices of good-quality streaky bacon, cooked, chopped and drained

For the dressing:

6 tbsp mayonnaise

½ lemon, zest and juice

1 tbsp chopped fresh chives

salt and freshly ground black pepper

1. To make the dressing, combine all the ingredients together in a bowl, check for seasoning and set aside.
2. To make the croutons, preheat the grill. Thinly slice the baguette on the diagonal into ½ cm slices. Brush both sides of each slice with olive oil and grill until golden brown. When still warm, rub one side with the raw garlic. Season with salt and pepper and set aside.
3. To make the salad, put the radicchio, iceberg lettuce, cherry tomatoes, sundried tomatoes and bacon into a bowl. Drizzle over some dressing and coat well. Turn out onto a salad platter.
4. Arrange the croutons around the sides, drizzle with additional dressing and serve.

 Add 2 finely sliced spring onions and replace the bacon with tuna.

Easy Coleslaw with a Creamy Horseradish Dressing

This is a different take on traditional coleslaw and is particularly good in the autumn and winter, when all the ingredients are in season. Sometimes I finely chop roasted beetroot instead of the shredded red cabbage, which is really tasty.

Serves 4

For the coleslaw:

2 tbsp sultanas

2 tbsp apple juice

2 celery stalks, diced

2 apples, peeled, cored and thinly sliced

¼ head red cabbage, very thinly sliced/shredded

¼ head Savoy cabbage, very thinly sliced/shredded

2 tbsp chopped fresh chives, plus extra to garnish

For the dressing:

4 tbsp mayonnaise

4 tbsp natural yoghurt

1 tbsp cream

1 tbsp horseradish sauce

½ lemon, zest and juice

salt and fresh ground black pepper

1. Soak the sultanas in the apple juice for about 30 minutes.
2. To make the dressing, place the mayonnaise, natural yoghurt, cream, horseradish sauce, lemon zest and juice in a bowl and stir to combine. Season with salt and pepper.
3. Toss the sultanas and the apple juice, celery, apples, shredded cabbage and chives with the dressing. Check the seasoning, adding salt and pepper to taste, and serve with some chopped chives scattered over to garnish.

 Use pears instead of the apples and sprinkle them with lemon juice to keep them from discolouring.

Feta, Mandarin and Wild Rice Salad

In our summer entertaining classes in the cookery school, we talk in detail about colour and texture and the shape and size of the components in a salad. Simply put, when compiling a salad, it's important to bear in mind that there should be an element of crunchiness, softness and attractive colour. Uneven shapes and sizes work best for holding the shape of the salad.

Serves 4

For the salad:

200g cooked wild rice

200g cooked white rice

4 spring onions, finely sliced

4 tbsp toasted and roughly chopped cashew nuts

1 x 400g tin of mandarins, drained, retaining a few to garnish

120g feta cheese, crumbled

2 tsp chopped fresh parsley

1 tsp chopped fresh basil

For the dressing:

1 orange, juice and zest

6 tbsp extra virgin olive oil

2 tbsp red wine vinegar

2 tbsp shredded fresh basil

1 tsp local honey

1 tsp wholegrain mustard

salt and freshly ground black pepper

1. To make the dressing, place all the ingredients in a jug and whisk to combine.
2. Combine the rice, spring onions, cashew nuts, most of the mandarins, the feta cheese and the herbs in a bowl.
3. Drizzle over enough vinaigrette to coat the rice mixture and place in a serving bowl. Place the remaining mandarins over the top. Place in the fridge for 30 minutes to allow the flavours to develop, then serve.

Try this with a crumbly blue cheese instead of the feta.

Warm BBQ Butternut, Red Onion and Spinach Salad with a Sesame Dressing

Char-grilling the butternut caramelises the sugars to give a lovely sweetness to this salad.
I turn this into a main course for lunch by adding bacon lardons and goat's cheese.

Serves 4

For the salad:

2 red onions, peeled and cut into wedges

1 butternut squash, peeled and sliced into wedges

extra virgin olive oil

salt and freshly ground black pepper

100g spinach, watercress or your favourite salad leaves

12–14 seedless red grapes

8 walnuts, roughly chopped

a few Parmesan shavings

For the dressing:

2 tbsp sesame oil

4 tbsp sunflower oil

1 tbsp white wine vinegar

1 tsp Dijon mustard

1 tbsp sesame seeds

salt and freshly ground black pepper

1. Place all the ingredients for the dressing into a bottle or jar with a lid and shake to combine.
2. Brush the onion and butternut squash wedges with a little oil and sprinkle over some salt and pepper. Place on a medium heat on the BBQ and roast for about 15–20 minutes, until soft. The onions will cook faster than the butternut squash.
3. In the meantime, toss the spinach and grapes together with some of the salad dressing and place on a large serving platter. Add the onion and butternut squash wedges. Sprinkle over the walnuts and the Parmesan shavings and drizzle a little more dressing over the top. Serve immediately.

❋ *As an alternative, try adding a few slices of mango instead of the grapes.*

Sweet and Sticky BBQ Glazed Sausages

I use this delicious glaze for chicken and pork chops too. It's so quick and easy to make, I feel like I'm cheating when I call it a recipe.

Serves 4

80g brown sugar

2 tbsp tomato ketchup

1 tsp Dijon mustard

12 pork sausages
(or chicken wings or drumsticks)

1. Preheat the BBQ to a medium heat.
2. Place the sugar, ketchup and Dijon mustard in a saucepan and heat on the hob, stirring frequently until the sugar dissolves.
3. Place the sausages on the BBQ over a medium heat (without the glaze) until they're almost cooked. Brush the sausages with the glaze and continue to grill until cooked through.

Due to the high sugar content in this recipe, a medium heat is necessary to ensure the glaze doesn't burn.

Gema's BBQ Pork

My friend Gema shared this recipe with me. It's a traditional BBQ marinade from her region in Lithuania, where they use it with pork shoulder. It's very effective in tenderising and sweetening the meat. I use pork fillet here, which needs less time to cook.

Serves 4–6

2 x 375g fillets of pork

For the marinade:

4 tbsp mayonnaise

4 tbsp tomato ketchup

1 tbsp white wine vinegar

5 tsp lemon juice

1 tsp salt

1 tsp sugar

1 tsp freshly ground black pepper

1. To prepare the pork, cut each fillet into 8 pieces. Place the slices of pork, cut side up, spaced out on a large piece of cling film. Cover with another layer of cling film. Using a meat mallet or rolling pin, hammer each piece of pork until you have an escalope. Remove the top layer of cling film.

2. To make the marinade, place all the marinade ingredients into a large bowl and whisk to combine. Toss the pork in the marinade, cover and refrigerate for about 2 hours, or better still, leave it overnight.

3. Preheat the BBQ to a medium heat. Place the pork escallopes on the BBQ and cook for about 3 minutes on each side, or until cooked through.

 This marinade does wonders for chicken thighs.

Smokey BBQ Ribs

Hands up – who doesn't like ribs? My children can't get enough of these. There's hardly any left over for the adults!

Serves 4

12 pork spare ribs, cut into 4 sections

extra virgin olive oil

For the marinade:

1 large red chilli, finely chopped

200ml balsamic vinegar

2 tbsp brown sugar

1 tbsp smoked paprika

1 tbsp tomato purée

salt and freshly ground black pepper

1. Place all the marinade ingredients in a saucepan and bring to the boil on the hob. Reduce the heat and simmer for 10 minutes, until it thickens. Allow to cool.
2. Coat the ribs with the marinade and leave for at least 3 hours.
3. Preheat the BBQ to a low heat. Shake off any excess marinade from the ribs, then grill the ribs for 30–40 minutes, depending on their size. Brush with the marinade every 10 minutes.
4. Once the ribs are cooked, leave them to rest for a few minutes. Cut into individual ribs and serve.

These can be served with Oven-roasted Chunky Chips (see p. 124) and salads of your choice.

Marinated T-bone Steak

Everybody loves a good steak and you can't beat a T-bone. It's the combination of the sirloin on one side and the fillet on the other, coupled with the marbling of the fat, that gives the meat its wonderful flavour.

Serves 4

4 x 350g T-bone steaks

4 tbsp extra virgin olive oil

2 garlic cloves, crushed

2 sprigs of rosemary

salt and freshly ground black pepper

1. Prepare the steaks by placing them in a shallow bowl with the oil, garlic and rosemary. Cover and marinate in the fridge for at least 2 hours or overnight. Bring to room temperature before cooking.
2. Preheat the BBQ to a high heat. Brush the rungs of the BBQ with the marinade.
3. Remove the steaks from the marinade and shake off any excess. Season both sides with salt and pepper and place immediately onto the BBQ.
4. Sear well on one side before turning. Cook to your preference and leave to rest for 2 minutes before serving.

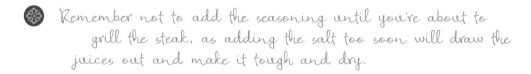 Remember not to add the seasoning until you're about to grill the steak, as adding the salt too soon will draw the juices out and make it tough and dry.

Cheesy Portobello Burgers

Vegetarians are always a little bit forgotten at the meat fest that a BBQ usually becomes, so you'll definitely score a few brownie points with these. Just be careful to keep the mushrooms away from all the meat – perhaps cook these first before the meat has hit the grill. You can always cook them on the griddle section of the BBQ or in a frying pan. Disposable trays are also useful for cooking in.

Makes 4

8 medium Portobello mushrooms, stalks removed and brushed

extra virgin olive oil

salt and freshly ground black pepper

4 tbsp pesto

4 artichoke hearts (from a jar)

1 jar of roasted red peppers

8 mozzarella slices

4 wholemeal baps, to serve

rocket leaves, to serve

1. Preheat the BBQ to a medium heat.
2. Brush the mushrooms with oil and season with salt and pepper. Spread 1 tbsp pesto on the bottom of each mushroom, then top with an artichoke heart, roasted peppers and mozzarella. Season lightly with additional salt and pepper to taste.
3. Brush the BBQ rungs with oil and place the mushrooms on top. Close the lid on the BBQ and leave to cook for 10–12 minutes.
4. Toast the baps on the BBQ. Serve 2 Portobello mushrooms on each bap, with rocket to garnish. Drizzle with a little oil to serve.

A good sundried tomato relish would be really nice with these.

149

Chicken Satay Sticks with Cucumber Salad

These chicken satay sticks are a real hit with my children. They can even be made on cocktail sticks and served with a satay dip as canapés. Here, we remove them from the skewers and place them in wraps.

Serves 4

4 skinless chicken breasts, cubed

1 red pepper, cut into 2cm dice

salt and freshly ground black pepper

sunflower oil

For the marinade:

100ml natural yoghurt

3 tbsp crunchy peanut butter

3 tbsp sweet chilli sauce

For the cucumber salad:

1 cucumber, halved lengthways, deseeded and thinly sliced

1 red onion, thinly sliced

1 lemon, juice only

1 tbsp Thai fish sauce (*nam pla*)

1 tbsp chopped fresh coriander leaves

To serve:

4 tbsp mayonnaise

4 tbsp mango chutney

4 flour tortilla wraps

1. First, soak 8 skewers if you are using wooden ones so they don't burn on the BBQ.
2. Place the natural yoghurt, peanut butter and sweet chilli sauce in a bowl and mix together. Add the cubed chicken and coat well. The chicken can be left in this marinade for 2–3 hours in the fridge or overnight.
3. To prepare the cucumber salad, mix together the cucumber, red onion, lemon juice, Thai fish sauce and coriander in a large bowl. Chill until ready to serve.
4. Preheat the BBQ to a medium heat.
5. Shake off any excess marinade from the chicken. Thread the chicken pieces onto the skewers, alternating with the diced red pepper. Season with salt and pepper.
6. Brush the BBQ rungs with oil. Place the skewers on the BBQ and cook, turning from time to time, until browned and cooked through.
7. Mix the mayonnaise with the mango chutney and spread on each of the wraps. Drain the cucumber and onion mixture and place in the centre of the wrap. Using 2 skewers for each wrap, slide off the diced chicken and red peppers and place on top of the cucumber salad. Roll up and serve immediately.

 Children like these served in soft hot dog rolls. Just remove the skewers first!

Picnic Loaf

This is my take on the Italian muffaletta. Inspired by my regular visits to Sicily and the wonderful ingredients available in the local markets, simply anything Italian goes here.

Serves 6

1 large loaf of crusty bread

120g tapenade

6 slices of ham

9 slices of mozzarella

9 slices of salami

9 slices of tomato

100g pesto

10 sundried tomato halves, roughly chopped

½ cucumber, thinly sliced

2 tbsp chopped capers

extra virgin olive oil

salt and freshly ground black pepper

1. Cut the top off the bread and scoop out the soft bread (keep this for making breadcrumbs later).
2. Spread the tapenade all around the inside of the loaf and on the inside of the removed top crust.
3. Create layers inside the bread (seasoning to taste as you go) with the ham, mozzarella, salami, tomatoes, pesto, sundried tomatoes, cucumber and capers. Repeat until you have used up all of the ingredients. Drizzle with extra virgin olive oil.
4. Replace the top of the bread and wrap the loaf with cling film. Place in the fridge overnight.
5. To serve, remove the cling film and cut into slices.

Make a vegetarian version by replacing the meats with marinated peppers, mushrooms and courgettes.

Quick Berry Ice Cream

There's nothing quite like homemade ice cream. OK, so the custard is shop bought, but everything else is homemade, and it's delicious!

Serves 6

500g mixed frozen berries

3 tbsp icing sugar

500ml store-bought thick custard

ice cream cones, to serve

1. Roughly chop the frozen berries in a food processor. Add the icing sugar and custard and blend again until the mixture is smooth.
2. Spoon into a container suitable for freezing. Freeze for 1 hour, or until just set. Remove from the freezer and scoop into cones or sandwich between 2 biscuits or wafers.

Adults can add a little kirsch to the mixture.

Peach and Hazelnut Yoghurt Lollies

These lollies are really easy to make and the children will love making them.

Serves 6–8

2 x 400g tins of peaches

500ml hazelnut yoghurt

2 tbsp icing sugar

1. Drain the juice from the peaches and finely chop them.
2. Place the yoghurt in a bowl and stir in the icing sugar. Fold in the peaches.
3. Spoon into ice lolly moulds, insert the lolly sticks and freeze.
4. To serve, dip the tip of the moulds into hot water for 2–3 seconds and carefully remove the frozen lollies.

 You can replace the peaches with 10 fresh strawberries.

Desserts

Five Quick
Sauces for Sweets

Do you ever find that you'd have the perfect dessert if only you had a tasty sauce to accompany it instead of always serving with a dollop of cream? These five quick ideas can be changed to suit your tastes. For example, replace the wasabi with orange zest, replace the frozen cranberries with raspberries and so on.

1 White Chocolate and Wasabi Sauce

150g white chocolate chips

60g butter

wasabi to taste (e.g. ¼ tsp)

1. Melt the chocolate and butter in a heatproof bowl set over a saucepan of simmering water. Gently stir in wasabi to taste.

2 Mocha Sauce

120g dark chocolate chips

75g butter

50ml espresso or very strong coffee

50ml cream

1. Melt the chocolate chips and butter in a heatproof bowl set over a saucepan of simmering water. Add the espresso and cream and stir to combine.

3 Creamy Peanut Sauce

100g crunchy peanut butter

200ml double cream

2 tbsp golden syrup

1. Heat all the ingredients in a saucepan until combined.

4 Marshmallow and Crème de Cassis Sauce

10 pink marshmallows

200ml cream

1 lemon, zest only

2 tbsp crème de cassis

1. Melt the marshmallows with the cream in a heatproof bowl set over a saucepan of simmering water. Stir in the lemon zest and crème de cassis.

5 Cranberry and Cointreau Sauce

100g dried cranberries

75g brown sugar

60ml water

2 tbsp Cointreau

1. Bring all the ingredients to the boil in a small saucepan and simmer for 2 minutes.

Thyme-infused Raspberry and Chocolate Meringue Tower

Everybody loves meringue and it's also a great standby if you have guests who are wheat intolerant. The tower effect creates that 'wow' factor when you serve it. The thyme-infused raspberries give an air of mystery to this dessert.

Serves 10–12

For the meringue:

6 egg whites

360g caster sugar

For the raspberries:

600ml red wine (that leaves a glass for the chef!)

4 tbsp honey

2 sprigs of thyme

700g raspberries

2 tsp arrowroot mixed with a little water, to thicken the sauce

For the filling:

300g dark chocolate

90g butter

150ml double cream, whipped

chocolate shavings (or a broken Flake bar), to decorate

thyme sprigs, to decorate

1. Preheat the oven to 140°C/fan 120°C/gas 1. Line a baking sheet with parchment paper. Draw large, medium and small heart shapes, measuring 24cm, 20cm and 16cm in length, on the underside of the parchment paper, ensuring that you can see the shape through the paper.

2. Place the egg whites in a spotlessly clean, dry bowl. With an electric hand mixer, whisk the egg whites until stiff but not dry. Gradually whisk in half of the caster sugar, a tablespoon at a time. Fold in the remaining sugar.

3. Spoon the meringue mixture into a piping bag with a plain nozzle. Secure the parchment paper to the baking sheet with a little of the meringue mixture to ensure the paper doesn't lift in the oven. Following the outline of the heart shapes, fill in the shapes.

4. Bake immediately for 1 ½ hours, or until set. When the meringues are done, leave them in the oven with the oven door slightly open so that the meringues can cool.

5. Meanwhile, to prepare the raspberries, place the red wine, honey and thyme in a saucepan and warm through. Remove from the heat and pour over the raspberries. Cool and place in the fridge for 30 minutes.

6. To make the filling, melt the chocolate and butter in a bowl over a pot of simmering water. Allow to cool, then fold in the whipped cream.

7. To make the sauce, gently remove the raspberries from the liquid with a slotted spoon, taking care not to break them,

and set aside. Strain the liquid through a sieve and return it to the saucepan. Add the arrowroot mixture and heat the liquid to thicken it to a light sauce consistency.

8. Spread the large and medium meringue hearts with some of the chocolate mixture and top with raspberries. Starting with the largest heart at the bottom, pile the meringues on top of each other.

9. Decorate with chocolate shavings and sprigs of thyme. Drizzle generously with the raspberry thyme sauce.

Replace the thyme with orange zest and the raspberries with blueberries for an alternative take on this lovely dessert.

Orange and Blueberry Cheesecake

I grew up on cheesecake – lemon cheesecake was one of my mother's signature desserts – so I just had to include a cheesecake here. This recipe contains two of your five a day, so start making it now!

Serves 10

For the base:

200g digestive biscuits

100g unsalted butter, melted

60g ground almonds

For the filling:

400g cream cheese

150g caster sugar

100ml sour cream

1 tsp orange zest

½ tsp orange essence

150ml double cream

250g blueberries, retaining a few to decorate

2 oranges, segmented, to decorate

1. Butter a 20cm springform tin.
2. To make the base, place the biscuits in a sealed plastic bag and crush them with a rolling pin. Alternatively, put them in a food processor with a metal blade and process until they resemble crumbs.
3. Place the biscuit crumbs, melted butter and ground almonds in a bowl and stir thoroughly until everything is combined. Press into the bottom of the buttered tin and chill in the fridge for at least 2 hours.
4. To make the filling, beat the cream cheese, sugar, sour cream, orange zest and orange essence together in a bowl until light and fluffy.
5. Whip the cream in a separate bowl until it forms soft peaks, then fold into the cream cheese mixture. Gently fold in most of the blueberries and spoon the mixture over the base.
6. Chill for at least 4 hours in the fridge, or until set. Decorate with the retained blueberries and orange segments and serve.

If orange essence isn't available, vanilla extract is lovely in this recipe too.

Mini Limoncello Mousse with Chilled Strawberries

How about this for a really easy grown-up dessert? It's a wonderful little tasting for a lighter option in the summer. It can easily be made without the limoncello for the kids.

Serves 4

200ml cream

100g mascarpone

1 lemon, zest only

4 tbsp icing sugar

3 tbsp limoncello

100g strawberries, chilled, to serve

4 shot glasses of limoncello, to serve (optional)

1. Lightly whip the cream.
2. Place the mascarpone in a bowl and add the lemon zest, icing sugar and limoncello. Mix to combine.
3. Gently fold the whipped cream into the limoncello mascarpone mix. Spoon into glasses and serve with chilled strawberries and a shot of limoncello.

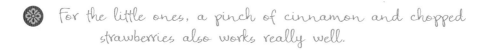 For the little ones, a pinch of cinnamon and chopped strawberries also works really well.

Creamy Nectarine and Blackberry Pots

A lovely healthy way to finish a meal. It's very light and the amaretti biscuits give it a beautiful flavour. It's also quick, as you use ready-made custard.

Serves 4

100g amaretti biscuits, crushed

4 tbsp finely chopped shelled pistachios, plus extra to decorate

250ml store-bought ready-made custard

250ml Greek yoghurt

2 tbsp lavender honey

4 ripe nectarines, stoned and finely sliced

175g blackberries

1. Mix the amaretti biscuits and pistachios together in a bowl.
2. Combine the custard, yoghurt and honey in a separate bowl.
3. Using dessert glasses, place a layer of the pistachio crumb mix in the base, followed by the nectarines, blackberries and the custard mix. Continue to layer, ending with a layer of custard mix. Decorate with some chopped pistachios.

This recipe can be adapted to use any fruit that you might have, such as apricots or pears. You can also change the nuts and use toasted chopped hazelnuts or pecans. Edible flowers or fresh mint leaves are another way to decorate this gorgeous dessert.

Fruity Lime Salad

I was experimenting with some light options to follow the traditional Christmas dinner, so I made this at Christmas for my family and it went down an absolute treat. I had the leftovers for breakfast with some local natural yoghurt, yum!

Serves 6

100g caster sugar

100ml water

2 star anise

2 limes, zest and juice

6 peaches, stoned and sliced

2 mangoes, peeled and cut into chunks

2 kiwi fruits, peeled and sliced

1 ripe pineapple, peeled, cored and diced

½ cantaloupe, peeled and sliced

fresh mint leaves, to decorate

1. To make the syrup, gently heat the sugar with the water and star anise in a small saucepan until the sugar dissolves. Bring to the boil and simmer, uncovered, for 4 minutes. Remove from the heat and add the lime zest and juice. Set aside.
2. Arrange all the fruit on a deep platter and pour the syrup over. Cover and chill for 1 hour to infuse the flavours. Decorate with mint leaves.

 I sometimes replace the lime with crushed lemongrass.

Orange Mocha Crème Brûlée

This is a very rich grown-up pudding that would be lovely served at a dinner party. The great thing is that it can be made in advance and left in the fridge until required, leaving you with the job of looking after your guests, safe in the knowledge that there is something delicious to look forward to.

Serves 6

4 tbsp cold espresso or very strong coffee

2 tbsp cocoa powder

2 oranges, zest only

9 egg yolks

75g golden caster sugar, plus extra to brûlée

450ml double cream

1. Preheat the oven to 140°C/fan 120°C/gas 1.
2. Blend the espresso with the cocoa powder and orange zest in a bowl. Add the egg yolks and sugar and stir. Pour the cream over the egg mixture and stir well.
3. Place a fine sieve on top of a large measuring jug and pour this mixture through the sieve into the jug. Then pour the mixture into 150ml coffee cups or ramekins, filling them three-quarters full.
4. Place the cups in a deep-sided roasting tray. Place the tray in the oven, then create a bain marie by pouring boiling water into the tray until it reaches halfway up the side of the cups. Cook for about 40 minutes.
5. To test if they're done, gently shake the tray. The brûlées should be just set while still having a slight wobble in the centre. Remove from the oven and allow to cool. Chill for 1 hour, or until firm.
6. Sprinkle the tops with the extra golden caster sugar. Use a kitchen blowtorch or place them under a really hot grill to brown.

❁ Make sure the coffee isn't too hot, as it could curdle the eggs.

Apricot, Date and Guinness Slices with Guinness Cream Sauce

This is my take on the traditional sticky toffee pudding recipe, adding a truly Irish dimension with the addition of the Guinness. We make this in our cookery school to great applause, though we find that the measurements of Guinness can be a bit heavy handed!

Makes 9 squares

For the slices:

150g stoned dates

120g dried apricots, chopped

150ml Guinness

120ml water

75ml whiskey

1 tsp bread soda (bicarbonate of soda)

175g Demerara sugar

85g butter, softened

3 medium eggs, beaten

180g self-raising flour

100g chopped walnuts

For the sauce:

75g butter

75ml Guinness

75ml double cream

2 tbsp runny honey

1. Preheat the oven to 200°C/fan 180°C/gas 6. Line a 21cm square brownie tin with parchment paper.
2. Put the dates, apricots, Guinness, water, whiskey and bread soda in a saucepan. Place over a gentle heat until the dates soften and break down, stirring occasionally. This should take about 4–5 minutes. Leave to cool.
3. Using an electric mixer, cream the sugar and butter until light and fluffy. Gradually beat in the eggs.
4. Fold the flour, walnuts and the cooled date mixture into the egg mix and transfer to the prepared tin. Bake for 35–40 minutes, until firm to the touch. Leave to cool in the tin for 5 minutes before turning out on a cooling rack. Cut into 9 squares.
5. To make the sauce, place the butter, Guinness, cream and honey in a saucepan and simmer over a low heat until the honey has dissolved and the sauce has thickened. Serve warm, drizzled over the slices.

 This sauce is delicious with ice cream and it freezes well too.

Five Ways
with Fruit Crumble

While crumbles are traditionally considered to be a rather simple dessert, the trick is to add your own touch, either to the topping or the fruit base. For example, some desiccated coconut is delicious added to the topping when making a mango crumble, while strawberry and cinnamon is a wonderful summer crumble base. There is a standard format for crumbles, and that is to cook the fruit with the sugar first to soften. Then place it in a gratin dish, top with your favourite crumble mix and bake until golden. Crumbles are extremely versatile, they freeze beautifully and are a great standby if you have unexpected guests. It's also a good way to use up surplus fruit. Double your crumble topping and freeze half in a freezer bag - it will keep for up to 3 months.

1 Apple and Mango Crumble

Serves 4–6

For the sauce:

3 large Golden Delicious apples, peeled, cored and diced

2 mangoes, peeled and diced

3 tbsp brown sugar

2 tbsp water

For the crumble:

65g plain flour

65g wholemeal flour

90g butter

65g brown sugar

65g oatmeal

5 walnuts, roughly chopped

natural yoghurt or ice cream, to serve

1. Preheat the oven to 190°C/fan 170°C/gas 5. Butter an ovenproof pie dish.
2. Place the apples, mangoes, brown sugar and water in a saucepan. Cover and cook for 5–10 minutes, until the fruit has softened.
3. Meanwhile, to make the crumble topping, place the plain and wholemeal flour in a mixing bowl. Rub in the butter with your fingertips until the mixture resembles breadcrumbs. Stir in the sugar, oatmeal and walnuts.
4. Spoon the fruit into the buttered ovenproof dish and sprinkle the crumble topping over the fruit. Bake for 20 minutes, until golden brown. Serve warm with a spoonful of yoghurt or your favourite ice cream.

2 Gooseberry and Elderflower Crumble

1kg gooseberries

2 tbsp elderflower syrup (see p. 196)

175g caster sugar, or to taste

3 Peach and Basil Crumble

8 peaches

4 basil leaves, finely chopped

100g caster sugar

4 Rhubarb and Ginger Crumble

1kg rhubarb

1 tsp ground ginger

200g caster sugar

5 Pear and Rosemary Crumble

8 pears, peeled and diced

1 large sprig of rosemary, leaves finely chopped

100g caster sugar

Ballyknocken Pecan Pudding

This is a magical pudding, as it creates its own sauce as it cooks. The pudding rises up and leaves behind a pool of buttery sauce. It's a lovely oven-to-table dessert. The trick is not to overcook it or the sauce will be absorbed back into the pudding.

Serves 8

225g self-raising flour

½ tsp salt

100g brown sugar, plus extra for sprinkling

1 egg

170ml milk

80g butter, melted and cooled

2 tbsp golden syrup

100g pecans, lightly toasted and chopped

For the sauce:

180ml boiling water

125g brown sugar

110g butter, melted

1 tsp vanilla extract

whipped cream, to serve

1. Preheat the oven to 180°C/fan 160°C/gas 4. Grease a 6cm- or 8cm-deep 2 litre ovenproof dish.
2. Sieve the flour and salt into a bowl. Stir in the brown sugar.
3. In a separate bowl, combine the egg, milk, melted butter and golden syrup. Whisk until smooth.
4. Add the egg mixture to the dry ingredients using a wooden spoon. Mix until smooth. Stir in the chopped pecans.
5. Spoon the batter into the greased dish. Smooth the top with a spatula and sprinkle extra brown sugar evenly over the batter.
6. To make the sauce, combine the boiling water, brown sugar, melted butter and vanilla in a jug. Carefully pour the sauce over the batter. As the pudding cooks, it rises and leaves behind a pool of buttery vanilla sauce.
7. Bake for 50–55 minutes, or until cooked through and an inserted skewer comes out clean. Leave to stand for 5 minutes. Serve with whipped cream.

You can add 4 tbsp rum to the sauce ingredients to give it a kick. Or zest an orange and add it to the batter mixture and use orange juice instead of water in the sauce ingredients to suit the younger palate.

Mini Chocolate Pots

I serve these to our B&B guests as part of a trio of desserts and they are incredibly more-ish. They look very attractive when a stencil is placed on top and dusted with icing sugar. Remove the stencil and serve.

Makes 10 espresso cups or 4 ramekins

200g dark chocolate

100g butter

2 eggs

2 medium egg yolks

4 tbsp caster sugar

2 tbsp ground almonds, plus extra for dusting

2 tbsp Baileys Irish Cream (optional)

icing sugar, to decorate

1. Preheat the oven to 180°C/fan 160°C/gas 4. Butter 10 espresso cups or 4 ramekins and dust with ground almonds. Shake out the excess.
2. Place the chocolate in a glass bowl over a saucepan of simmering water to melt.
3. Melt the butter separately and pour over the chocolate. (This will ensure the chocolate melts quicker.)
4. Whisk the whole eggs, egg yolks and sugar together in a bowl until light and pale in colour. Gently fold in the chocolate mixture, ground almonds and Baileys (optional).
5. Divide the mixture between the espresso cups, filling them until they're three-quarters full. Bake for 15–20 minutes, until risen and just set (longer if using ramekins). Dust with icing sugar and serve.

The pots can be prepared up to 4 hours in advance and kept uncooked in the fridge, but a few extra minutes will need to be added to the cooking time.

Blueberry and Pear Clafoutis

Have fun with this 'shake and bake' clafoutis. The liquid batter ingredients can be placed in a jar and shaken before being incorporated into the dry ingredients.

Serves 6

350g pears, peeled and quartered and sprinkled with lemon juice

125g blueberries

50g icing sugar

25g flour

4 eggs, beaten

250ml cream

vanilla ice cream, to serve

1. Preheat the oven to 180°C/fan 160°C/gas 4. Butter a 1.2 litre baking dish.
2. Add the prepared fruit to the dish.
3. Sieve the icing sugar and flour into a bowl. Gradually whisk in the eggs until smooth. Whisk in the cream. (Alternatively, have some fun making the batter by pouring the beaten eggs and cream into a jar and shaking well, then whisk into the flour and icing sugar.) Pour the mixture over the fruit, ensuring that all the fruit is covered.
4. Bake for 30–40 minutes, until light golden brown. To test if it's done, gently shake the dish. The clafoutis should be just set while still having a slight wobble in the centre. Allow to cool for about 15 minutes. Serve with vanilla ice cream.

Try this with pitted cherries instead – it's equally delicious and easy.

Apple Berry Jelly

For my children's birthday parties, I fill large Duplo-type blocks with this jelly mix. To remove the jelly, I dip the blocks upside down in hot water for a split second and then turn out.

**Serves 6–8
(using small plastic
glasses or moulds)**

100g sugar

150ml water

4 sheets of leaf gelatine

300ml apple juice

120g mix of strawberries, raspberries and blueberries, washed and hulled and halved if necessary, plus extra to decorate

fresh mint, to decorate

1. Pour the sugar and water into a saucepan and heat, stirring, until the sugar has dissolved. Do not allow to boil.
2. Meanwhile, soak the gelatine in a little cold water for about 1 minute, or until soft. Remove the sheets from the water and add them to the warm syrup. Whisk until the gelatine has dissolved. Allow to cool slightly. Transfer to a jug and add the apple juice.
3. Place a few berries into the bottom of each glass/mould and pour in the jelly mix. Place in the fridge to set. Decorate with a few berries and mint.

To keep the berries at the bottom of the glass, pour some of the liquid over, then place in the fridge for 1 hour to set. Take out and pour over the remaining liquid. This is also delicious with orange juice and peaches.

Cherry and Lemon Trifle

It has probably come to your attention that a lot of my desserts have fruit incorporated into them – my children say it's the 'good cop, bad cop' coming out in me. But I do believe that all desserts benefit form the addition of fruit for flavour, texture and lightness … although chocolate is great on its own! For the kids, replace the kirsch with slightly diluted blackcurrant cordial.

Serves 4–6

1 x 397g tin of
condensed milk

1 lemon, zest and juice

6 tbsp lemon curd

200ml double cream,
whipped

1 x 400g tin of Morello
cherries, pitted (reserve
a few to decorate)

4 tbsp kirsch

16–20 ladyfinger biscuits

edible flowers
(e.g. calendula or pansies),
to decorate

1. Combine the condensed milk, lemon zest and juice and lemon curd in a bowl, then fold in the whipped cream.
2. Drain the tin of black cherries and retain the juice. Add the kirsch to the cherry juice in a bowl and dip the ladyfingers in the mixture.
3. Place a few cherries into individual serving glasses. Continue with a layer of ladyfingers that have been dipped in the kirsch mixture. Spoon over the lemon cream mix. Continue layering, finishing with the lemon cream.
4. Chill for a minimum of 1 hour in the fridge to allow the flavours to blend. Bring to room temperature before serving. Decorate with the reserved cherries and edible flowers.

✻ Replace the lemon curd and fresh lemon with Nutella and chopped hazelnuts. Having lived in southern Germany for a year, I developed a taste for Black Forest Gateau and it never tasted quite the same at home. This is my take on a lighter version of the German classic.

Drinks

Elderflower Cocktail

Some Austrian guests to our B&B shared this recipe with me, although they used white wine. To pay homage to the Sicilian side of the family, naturally I started to experiment with Prosecco and I can honestly say it's delicious.

Serves 6

1 bottle of Prosecco

12 frozen elderflower syrup cubes

6 sprigs of lemon balm

1. Prepare the elderflower syrup as per the recipe below and freeze in ice cube trays.
2. To serve, pour the Prosecco into champagne flutes and top with 2 cubes of elderflower syrup and a sprig of lemon balm.

Elderflower Syrup

Early June is elderflower season and it comes and goes so quickly. Not only do elderflowers produce such delicious results, but I love the time spent foraging on our farm with my family. And for some reason, the sun is usually shining here in Wicklow at that time too!

Makes 500ml

500g caster sugar

500ml cold water

10 elderflower heads, stalks removed

1 lemon, zest and juice

1 ½ tbsp citric acid

sparkling water, to serve

1. Make a sugar syrup by placing the sugar and water in a saucepan over a low heat. Stir until the sugar dissolves. Remove from the heat and leave to cool.
2. Place the elderflower heads, lemon zest and juice and citric acid in a bowl along with the sugar syrup. Stir, cover and leave for 2 days. Strain into sterilised glass bottles or freeze in an ice cube tray or bags.
3. To serve, pour about 1 ½ tbsp of the elderflower syrup into a glass and top up with sparkling water.

Pink Lemonade

What a lovely summer drink and a good change from fizzy drinks. It only keeps for a week, but I think you'll find that it'll be gone before that! At first, you might find that little boys are not so enamoured with the pink hue, but once they taste it, they love it.

Makes 350ml syrup

1 ½ lemons

1 orange

500g fresh raspberries

300g caster sugar

350ml cold water

ice, mint and sparkling water, to serve

1. Squeeze the juice from the lemons and orange.
2. Place the lemon and orange juice, raspberries, sugar and cold water in a saucepan. Bring to the boil, reduce the heat and simmer for 2 minutes. Turn off the heat and leave to cool.
3. Pass through a sieve, pressing the contents with the back of a spoon to extract all the juice. Store in sterilised glass bottles for up to 1 week in the fridge.
4. To serve, pour about 1 ½ tbsp (or to taste) of the lemonade syrup into a glass and top up with still or sparkling water, ice and mint.

For a shortcut version, mix cranberry juice with homemade lemonade syrup and cold water to dilute.

Watermelon and Cinnamon Rum Cocktail

This is a great summer party drink. Most recipes discard the watermelon – what a waste, it's one of your five-a-day!

Makes 15 cocktails

1 small watermelon, peeled, deseeded and cubed

3 whole cinnamon sticks

750ml Bacardi

lemonade, lime wedges and ice cubes, to serve

1. Place the watermelon in a large jug or bowl. Add the cinnamon sticks and Bacardi and cover tightly. Place in the fridge for 7 days to allow the flavours to blend.
2. Strain the watermelon and cinnamon sticks and pour the liquid into sterilised glass bottles.
3. Serve in tall glasses mixed with lemonade, lime wedges and lots of ice – and maybe a cocktail umbrella on the side!

Blend the leftover watermelon with sugar, freeze and serve as a dessert course.

Pear Royale

This is a lovely celebration drink. Everybody loves a bit of bubbly, but be warned, it's strong stuff!

Serves 6

2 fresh pears, peeled, cored and sliced

75g sugar

150ml water

2 tbsp brandy

1 bottle of Prosecco, chilled

1. Poach the pears in the sugar and water. When softened, remove the pears from the poaching liquid and allow to cool.
2. Place the cooled pear slices in champagne glasses or wine goblets and pour over the brandy.
3. When ready to serve, top up with Prosecco.

✽ Other fruit can be used, such as raspberries, strawberries or fresh peaches.

Index

207